Building Britain's Wooden Walls

Orion   Goliath   Zealous   Thesus   Le Guervier Audacious Le Conquérant   Le Spartiate

The above painting by Mark Myers, *RSMA, FASMA* was commissioned
by the author and shows Nelson's fleet on the evening of 1 August 1798
turning and breaking the French line of battle which stretched across
the mouth of Aboukir Bay. The relative positioning of the vessels
shown has been gleaned from the log books of the vessels concerned.

Building Britain's Wooden Walls

The Barnard Dynasty c. 1697 – 1851

John E. Barnard

Anthony Nelson

First published in 1997 by Anthony Nelson
P.O. Box 9, Oswestry, Shropshire SY11 1BY, England

ISBN 0 904614 63 8

Designed by Harold Bartram, London
Layout by Quetzal Communications, Basingstoke
Printed in Great Britain by Redwood Books, Trowbridge,
Wiltshire

Jacket picture: "A view from The Waters of Messrs Barnard and
Dudman's Shipyard, Deptford" – John Cleveley 1774

End papers: A composite painting by John Cleveley (1712-77)
showing the *Hampshire* on her building stocks at Johns Ness,
the *Biddeford* being towed from Ipswich to Harwich for
rigging and in the foreground, the bomb-ship *Granado*

Contents

Acknowledgements   1

Foreword   2

Author's Note   4

Introduction   5

Chapter I   John Barnard the Elder c 1665-1716   8

Chapter II   John Barnard the Younger c 1705-1784   11

Chapter III   The King's Yard Harwich 1742-1748   17

Chapter IV   The King's Yard Harwich 1748-1763   23

Chapter V   The King's Yard Harwich 1763-1776   30

Chapter VI   The King's Yard Harwich 1776-1783   33

Chapter VII   William Barnard 1762-1763   37
                  Partnership with William Dudman at
                  the Nova Scotia Yard and at the Grove St
                  Partnership, Deptford

Chapter VIII   The Hon East India Company   41

Chapter IX   The Grove St Partnership 1763-1772   45

Chapter X   The Grove St Partnership 1772-1779   47

Chapter XI   Deptford Green and Grove St 1780-1790   51

Chapter XII   Deptford Green and Grove St 1790-1795   59
                  Dissension and Dissolution

Chapter XIII   Frances Barnard, Sons & Co 1795-1805   63

Chapter XIV   Edward George Barnard 1805-1851   70

                  Epilogue   77

                  Addendum   78

                  Appendices I to XVIII   81

                  Notes and References   104

                  Bibliography   106

                  Picture Credits   107

                  Index   108

To my wife
Georgina

Acknowledgements

It is certainly no easy task to properly thank all those who have contributed to the writing of this book - and there were many. Private individuals, Family History Societies, Local Record Offices, Libraries, the PRO and Museums all gave unstinted assistance. Throughout the years of my research the generosity of my correspondents in devoting both time and labour knew no bounds. I thank them all.

I must, nevertheless, give special thanks to a selected few: to Hugh Moffat for the wealth of detail he supplied in respect of the family's early shipbuilding days at Ipswich and the Upper Orwell: to David Butcher for providing me with the genealogy of the Barnard family of shipbuilders of Lowestoft: to Dr John Bevan for his uncanny knack of unearthing most interesting snippets of information from the most unlikely places: to Marian Sartin for the depth of her research, especially into the genealogy of the later and more remote members of the Barnard family: to Brian Lavery and Pieter van der Merwe of the National Maritime Museum, Greenwich for reading the final draft and suggesting certain alterations and additions. On the technical side of production thanks are due to Mark and Ian Dicken for their back-up assistance in the field of computers.

Jean Sutton, authoress of the highly acclaimed 'Lords of the East', has earned my everlasting gratitude in not only writing the Foreword to this work but also in reading the chapter on the Hon East India Company and in making suggestions for its betterment.

Finally I must thank my wife Georgina without whose co-operation this book could never have been written. As a maid of all work she became my fellow researcher: as secretary she spent many hours at her word processor brilliantly transcribing the almost indecipherable text of my manuscript: as chauffeuse she was called upon to make sudden and unexpected return journeys to London. Her understanding and dedication assured the completion of the project, which in itself gave us a new life in which we have formed numerous friendships both at home and abroad.

Foreword

Notwithstanding Philip Banbury's admirable work "Shipbuilders of the Thames and Medway", until now the student of merchant shipbuilding has had to be satisfied with statistics - and those imperfect - while naval historians have steadfastly ignored the merchant yards' massive contribution to Britain's supremacy at sea in the 19th century. Now Mr Barnard introduces us to four generations of real men grappling with everyday problems. His choice of the word 'dynasty' is inspired: this research reveals that the shipbuilding members of the Barnard family were princes in their field: hardworking, highly skilled craftsmen; excellent managers and entrepreneurs; leading merchant shipbuilders both in Suffolk and on the Thames for almost a century.

On the outbreak of war with Spain in 1739, and later France, the Navy Board turned to merchant yards for the additional resources and flexibility required to produce the naval vessels demanded in increasing numbers. British policy remained consistent throughout the decades that followed: control of the seas. The French government lent ships, equipment and money for the support of its renowned privateers who wrought havoc among our merchant shipping, but it was the country which controlled the seas that claimed the final victory.

Between 1600 and 1834 approximately 1400 East Indiamen were built at an average burthen of 500 tons, far larger than any other merchant vessels. About twenty such ships sailed annually from England carrying chests of silver dollars to buy the luxuries of the lands beyond the Cape of Good Hope. This trade was a monopoly of the East India Company. The ship lists given in Appendix XVII show that the Barnard family built 77 naval vessels between the years 1740 and 1813 and 62 East Indiamen between the years 1763 and 1825. Building Indiamen and naval vessels in the same yard was a happy marriage. They were of similar scantling - this work shows that conversions were fairly common - and were built according to analogous contracts. Payment in each case was by instalment at agreed stages of construction. Mr Barnard's research reveals an easy relationship between the merchant builders and the naval dockyard officials, understandable since there was much movement between the two. The Navy Board officials frequently offered a helping hand, even with the construction of Indiamen: perhaps not surprising since these ships fulfilled the role of an arm of the Navy in the eastern seas throughout the prolonged struggle with both the French navy and the redoubtable privateers.

Circumstances favoured the River builders to a remarkable degree from the mid- eighteenth century to the close of the Napoleonic wars in 1815. Though naval contracts were very lucrative for the merchant builder when all went well, there were many pitfalls which could bring disaster in their wake, as the experience of John Barnard the Younger at Harwich shows. The Thames builders were protected against these reverses by their East India contracts. Payments for East Indiamen were regular and generous. The owners' monopoly of the East India Company's supply of shipping, described by Mr Barnard, insulated them from any downward pressure on freight rates.

In 1763 nearly a quarter of a century of war came to an end, and with it the cessation of profitable naval contracts. This period exactly coincided with developments within the East India Company that resulted in a boom in India shipbuilding. Investment in an East Indiaman had never been a purely commercial consideration, but a source of patronage, and patronage was power in the political climate of mid-eighteenth century Britain. The number of new East Indiamen proliferated, bringing a good deal of work to the Thames yards just at the time naval contracts fell off. For those familiar with shipbuilding the message was clear. The future was East Indiamen, and that meant the Thames. The momentous decisions made by William Barnard, William Dudman and Henry Adams must be representative of those made by many other shipbuilders, contributing to the great increase in merchant yards along the Thames in the latter half of the eighteenth century.

In the late 1760s it was revealed that the Company was grossly over supplied with shipping and ships were for some time employed on a rota system, each ship resting for one year after each voyage - a circumstance which has given rise to the myth that a voyage to the east lasted three years when it actually took eighteen months.

This costly state of affairs was brought to an end by an Act of Parliament in 1772 which provided for the cessation of new building of Indiamen until the Company's shipping was reduced to 45,000 tons. Circumstances again favoured the Thames builders. By the time those Indiamen already on the stocks were launched the Navy Board was again seeking contracts to meet the fresh emergency presented by the American War of Independence which began in 1775, when Britain again faced the French might at sea - now greatly enhanced and refined.

Immediately following the cessation of hostilities and the consequent reduction in naval contracts, the Commutation Act of 1784 slashed the duty on tea, eliminating the smuggling trade at a stroke, and effectively doubling the amount of China tea imported into Britain. Even before the formal introduction by the Company in 1793 of a new class of 36 ships of 1000 tons to meet this new situation, the owners had responded by placing contracts with the merchant yards for large ships. This is reflected in William Barnard's list of Indiamen launched after 1787; Frances Barnard Sons and Co and Edward George Barnard built several of the new class between 1795 and 1825. These years saw the resumption of naval contracts which reached record levels between 1793 and 1815 in the final bout of the struggle for world supremacy between Britain and France.

Fortune at last stopped smiling on the Thames shipbuilders in the first quarter of the nineteenth century. Several streams converged to produce a river which washed away two centuries of privilege enjoyed by the East India shipowners, and consequently by the merchant builders. Government support enabled the Company's directors to resist the owners' demands for freight rates which had become scandalously high; government pressure also ensured the admittance of cheaper and better India built shipping to Europe; the 'new shippers' of the outports broke the River builders' monopoly; coppering doubled an Indiaman's life; and the greatest blow - the ending of the Company's monopoly of trade with India introduced competition with all its attendant economies. All these were elements in the eventual decline of production on the River which would be hidden by the prodigious output of naval ships until the close of the Napoleonic wars.

Edward George Barnard's business was representative of many of the River builders. By 1825 most of the old firms had gone out of business, and not until mid-century would a new breed of enterprising and entrepreneurial men - engineers - bring glory again to the Thames.

John Barnard's work will be welcomed by the growing numbers of students of maritime history who recognize the merchant shipbuilders' contribution to our national heritage on two counts: the East Indiamen who developed the world trade routes and the naval vessels which protected them. Both have until now been shamefully ignored. John Barnard's work begins the task of redressing the balance.

Jean Sutton

Author's Note

The research which preceded the writing of this book was inspired by chance rather than design.

A fortuitous discovery in the waiting-room of my oculist in 1985 set the wheels in motion. Idly turning the pages of a glossy magazine, I came across a coloured print of a wooden merchantman on her stocks. The caption read 'An Indiaman in Mr Barnard's Yard, Deptford published by H. Moses 1824' (see picture above). Stimulated by this unexpected find and with my curiosity whetted by the size and importance of the vessel shown, I decided to investigate. It was a decision which I have never regretted. For although my self-imposed task took longer to complete and proved more onerous than expected, the rewards more than compensated for the time and trouble involved.

My research quickly disclosed that very little had been published concerning the merchant shipbuilders of the eighteenth and early nineteenth centuries, and of the important role these relatively small family businesses played in providing ships of war for His Majesty's service and merchantmen for the shipping interests of the Honourable East India Company. Furthermore, I found that what little had been published often consisted of incomplete ship lists and an occasional genealogical table of the families involved.

My primary aim in writing this book has been to put flesh and blood on the bare bones of statistical evidence and to present the routine business lives of the eighteenth and early nineteenth century private merchant shipbuilders through the eyes of four generations of the Barnard family. In principle I have avoided writing a genealogical study of the Barnards *per se.*, an approach which would inevitably be of little more than family concern. The premise of the work is that the Barnard experience has wider implications and interest; for the problems they faced and the successes they achieved would, in the main, have been common to their fellow-builders in the industry. They are, in short, taken as an epitome of their time and profession, and the fate which befell the last members of the Barnard shipbuilding line is recorded in the Epilogue and in an Addendum.

Much of the information concerning the routine and work of the yards results from a study of the original Barnard letters to the Navy Board held by the Public Record Office. In order to retain the personal element

and the distinctive eighteenth century flavour of the letters I have, wherever possible, allowed the writers to relate incidents in their own words by extensive quotation. A great deal of the atmosphere of the age is lost, I believe, in attempting to paraphrase eighteenth century letters in modern terms.

Although the work contains much statistical data and lifts the veil on the working practices of the day it is also anecdotal in a way which may be peripheral to the central theme but aims to set it within the social, economic and maritime issues of the times. There is much in the text and the statistical information which will, I hope, interest students. However, it is mainly directed at that body of readers who, although having an inherent interest in the maritime history of this country, has scant knowledge of the private shipbuilding enterprise which, in a relatively short period, contributed to Britain gaining mastery of the seas. The Barnard family of shipbuilders rose to prominence in the eighteenth century when the European powers were engaged in conflict on the continent of Europe and were, at the same time, battling for supremacy on the high seas.

It is my sincere hope that the professional story of the Barnard family will draw attention to the lack of exposure which has so far been given to the important element which they represent in Britain's great maritime past. The many similar family businesses may, individually, have been relatively small undertakings; but the combined output of their yards provided the ships which assured success both for the Royal Navy and for that doughty commercial breed of men who opened up the ocean trade routes of the world to British business.

Introduction
Merchant Shipbuilding in the Eighteenth Century

Wooden walls

The designation wooden walls, often used to define the fleets of maritime nations prior to the invention of the propeller and iron-clad, has its history in ancient literature. Herodotus, 484-425 BC in his History (BK.7 Ch.141-3) quoted the following proclamation from the Delphic Oracle.

Then far seeing Jove grants this to the prayers of Athenê:
Safe shall the wooden wall continue for thee and thy children
Wait not the tramp of the horse, nor the footmen mightily moving
Over the land, but turn your back to the foe and retire ye

The Delphic Oracle spoke in riddles which were open to a number of different interpretations. It was Themistocles, a leading Athenian citizen, who counselled his countrymen to be ready to fight on board their ships – the wooden walls – in which their god, through the Oracle, had told them to put their trust.

The growth of naval power in the reigns of George II and III necessary to meet the ever-changing pattern of world events was reflected in the size of the British fleet, which over a period of only 76 years increased four-fold. At the outbreak of hostilities with Spain in 1739, commonly known as the War of Jenkins's Ear the fleet consisted of some 240 vessels; in 1815, with the defeat of Napoleon at Waterloo, the number had risen to over 1000. The period is hailed as one of the most momentous in the maritime history of this country and the patriotic fervour of the age is epitomised in the words of such songs as 'Rule Britannia' and 'Hearts of Oak'. The laurels of victory were not, however, won without a bitter struggle, and one in which the naval vessels built in the merchant yards played a key role in determining the outcome.

In addition to the expansion of the Navy in this period the merchant shipbuilder also profited from the growth of world trade, in which the East India Company played a significant part, both in the amount of goods carried and in the number and excellence of its vessels.

It was, therefore, a capricious turn of fate which determined that in the second decade of the nineteenth century both sources of demand for ships lapsed. The defeat of Napoleon in 1815 and the Government's abolition of the East India Company's monopoly of the India trade in 1813 brought an abrupt end to years of affluence. The merchant shipbuilders had enjoyed to the full the long wave of prosperity but when the tide of fortune turned they found themselves stranded on a barren shore and in an inhospitable climate, from which few escaped unscathed.

The merchant builders of the times were, for the most part, small family businesses, operating from yards or building slips found on the estuaries, rivers, inlets and creeks of the British Isles. Many of the sites were of considerable antiquity, with working histories probably dating back to the time when the area was first settled by man. They were simple in the extreme, needing only an area capable of accommodating a woodpile, saw-pits (preferably covered), a forge or smith's shop, sundry sheds and, most important of all, a firm, gently-sloping beach leading into a sufficient depth of water to float and manoeuvre a vessel when launched. Prior to the seventeenth century ships were built by rule of thumb, fathers passing on to their sons the secrets of the shipbuilder's art.

The Royal Dockyards, inaugurated by Henry VIII, were in principle expected to build, repair, refit, arm and victual His Majesty's ships of war at all times. In practice this proved difficult, for when emergencies arose which called for substantial additions to the fleet the Royal Yards had neither the capacity nor the flexibility to comply with the demands made upon them; a situation which resulted in the employment of merchant builders. Nevertheless the Royal Dockyards continued to build the largest vessels; which were those classified as first rate or second rate ships of the line.

The term 'ships of the line' was coined in the late seventeenth century when, with the improvement in fire-power, the age-old practice of individual ship-to-ship combat was superseded by a more orderly form of

NAMES of each particular Part of a new Ship, as they are put together (in a progreſſive Manner) for Frameing and Finiſhing the Structure Building on the Stocks.

Part	Page	Part	Page	Part	Page
Keel	85	Breaſt Hooks	22	Scuttles	143
Stem	160	Fore Step	160	Gratings	66
Sternpoſt (Framed and raiſed together)	161	Riders	132	Ladders	88
Tranſoms	174	Pointers	121	Manger	103
Faſhion Pieces	54	Crotches	47	Pallating Magazine and Bread-room	114
Dead Riſing	49	Steps Main, Mizon, Main Capſton	160		
Floor	57			Gunwales	68
Timbers	171	Decks Lower the, Flat or Plank	50	Rails	128
Keelſon	85			Gangways	63
Futtocks	61	Orlop	113	Cleats	35
Hawſe Pieces	72	Capſtons	28	Kevels	86
Top Timbers	172	Pillars	118	Ranges	129
Waals	181	Channels	32	Knight Heads	87
Harpings	71	Navel Hoods	110	Rother	137
Plank	120	Knee, Cheeks of the Head	86	Tiller	170
Clamps	35		33	Scuppers	143
Sleepers	153	Lyon	102	Standards	158
Foot Waaling	57	Trailboard	173	Rufftrees	139
Beams	6	Gallery	62	Poop Lanterns	89
Knees	87	Taffarel	168	Cradle or Buildgeways (For Launching)	44
Bitts, Croſs Pieces	10	Quarter Pieces	127		23
Carlings	29	Brackets	21		
Ledges	93	Well	185		
Waterways	183	Pumps	124	N.B. All the foregoing Particulars, upon any Emergency, may, be taken in Hand very nearly together.	
Spirketing	156	Limber Boards	97		
Upper Deck	50	Garboard Strake, or Plank	63		
String	165				
Quarter Deck	50	Bulkheads	23		
Forecaſtle	58	Ports	122		
Partners Maſt, Capſton	116	Cathead	30		
		Cheſtrees	34		
Comeings	40	Hatchways	72		

From 'A Naval Expositor' by T.R. Blanckley 1750

warfare. Protagonists developed a tactic whereby opposing fleets formed line astern and, sailing on parallel courses, attempted to destroy the overall strength of the enemy formation by the discharge of their broadside armaments. This called for the stoutest of vessels and crews of the highest calibre. By the time of Nelson only vessels of the first rate, second rate and third rate were usually nominated ships of the line.

The concept of 'rating' or categorizing His Majesty's ships, according to either their size or some other factor, was not new and by the beginning of the eighteenth century it had become customary to do so according to the armament carried. In 1741 a vessel armed with 100 guns was graded as a 1st rate, whilst those with 90 guns were 2nd rates; a 3rd rate vessel carried anything between 80 and 64 guns and 4th rates between 50 and 58 guns. Vessels graded as 5th rates, known as frigates, carried 20 guns and possessed superior sailing qualities. Lesser vessels came under the heading of 6th rates. Special craft such as bomb-vessels were not rated but were classified according to their functions. With the passing of time and improvements in technology the armament carried by all vessels increased.

Historically the practice of employing private or merchant builders for the construction of naval ships had always engendered a great deal of dissension and in the late seventeenth and early eighteenth centuries the Navy Board was still strongly opposed to the principle of having naval vessels built other than in the Royal Dockyards. For instance, in 1699 Edmund Dummer, Surveyor of the Navy, gave it as his opinion that:

'Among the many abuses that have crept into the Navy, a very dangerous custom is in the building of ships by contract and over and above the exorbitant profits arising from such contracts are those arising from bad materials and bad workmanship, so that in time of action contract ships are proved to be no way at all to answer the uses of the Navy... such ships... are worn out in less than half the time those built in the King's Yards.'

The services of the merchant builders were not required for the greater part of the first half of the eighteenth century and it was not until the outbreak of the war with Spain in 1739 that the Navy Board resorted to calling for the output of the merchant yards. From then on the practice increased, until, in the period 1756-1815, more ships of the line were built in merchant yards than in the Royal Dockyards.

The building of these great vessels called for the employment of a number of trades, mostly encompassed within the word shipwright, a qualification only gained after an apprenticeship of either seven or nine years. A 74-gun ship took some three to four years to complete, including a period set aside for seasoning the hull in frame. A merchant builder with a Navy Board contract was responsible only for the hull: the masts being stepped and rigging added later, probably in a Royal Yard.

With modern assembly techniques in mind it is difficult to appreciate that shipbuilders in the eighteenth century (and before) built a vessel from the keel up entirely from raw materials delivered to the yard. Tree trunks, complete with bark, were transported straight from the forest to the site, where they were seasoned, stacked, sawn, shaped and carved into the multitude of patterns required. The number of individual parts necessary to build a single vessel could be counted in thousands rather than hundreds.

The amount of timber required for the construction of, say, a 74-gun ship, is estimated as the product of approximately 3000 fully-grown oak trees, English oak being the Navy Board's preference. Not surprisingly a dramatic increase in demand for oak, from 320,000 tons in 1760 to 700,000 tons in 1805, brought in its train severe shortages, which were partially satisfied by the import of American white oak from New Brunswick and Quebec. Nevertheless, the search for and procurement of a sufficient supply of oak of the required quality to meet both current and future demand remained a problem throughout the period. The masts required to rig the fleet also called for an ever increasing quantity of pine from the Baltic - known as the East Countries. Later in the eighteenth century the massive white pine from the virgin forests of North America helped alleviate the shortage.

The question of adequate finance was a constant source of concern to the smaller merchant builder, for a 74-gun ship cost something in excess of £23,000 - a sum which the builder would often find difficult to raise from his own resources. The expenditure would, of course, be spread over a building period of, say, three years, which allowed the Navy Board to adopt a payment by instalment procedure. The first instalment was paid on the signing of the contract, to be followed perhaps by six further instalments of the same amount at agreed stages of construction. A final payment, known as the 'perfect payment', was made on delivery of the vessel into the hands of the Navy Board, which in practice was the day of the launch. Although, in principle, the instalment system appeared fair to both parties, the actual method of payment adopted by the Navy Board left much to be desired in that the merchant builders received Navy Bills in settlement of monies due. All was well when the Navy Board had sufficient funds in hand to back the Bills it issued; but owing to the reluctance of Parliament to vote sufficient money for the maintenance of the fleet, especially in times of peace, the Treasury was, more often than not, short of the necessary cash. The merchant builder received instead a Bill with an unstated date of payment, with a miserly entitlement for the holder to receive interest, pending encashment, at the rate of 4%

per annum. Not surprisingly Navy Bills were not popular in the money markets of the day, which resulted in merchant builders being forced to accept swingeing discounts on them to obtain prompt encashment.

The Navy Board was a Board of Commissioners established in 1546 by Henry VIII and was part of the structure of naval administration, which in itself consisted of a number of Boards responsible for varying aspects of naval matters. They, in turn, were subordinate to the Board of the Admiralty. The Navy Board was responsible for the ordering, building, repair, refitting, victualling and manning of all naval. vessels, whilst the Board of Admiralty was, among other things, responsible for naval strategy.

Contracts granted to merchant builders tended to generate a great deal of correspondence and although letters from the Navy Board have in the main been lost, those from the merchant builders to the Board were carefully filed at the time of receipt and are still available for inspection. The ravages of time have taken their toll on the number originally filed but over 200 Barnard letters have survived, making it possible to gain an insight into the day-to-day life of an eighteenth century merchant builder.

Chapter I

John Barnard The Elder c.1665 - 1716

'I am credibly informed, that that Mystery of Shipwrights for some descents hath been preserved successively in families, of whom the Petts about Chatham are of singular regard; good success have they with their skill, and carefully keep so precious a pearl, lest otherwise amongst many friends some foes attain unto it. It is no monopoly which concedeth that from common enemies, the conceding whereof, is for the common good. May this Mystery of Shipbuilding in England never he lost till this floting (sic) world be arrived at its own Haven, the End and Dissolution thereof.'

Thomas Fuller. History of Worthies of England. 1662 [(1)]

The Barnard family was in all probability the product of such a mould; for although there is no indication of when and where the first member of the family became party to the art and science of shipbuilding, their roots lay deep in East Anglia's shipbuilding past. There was certainly a family of shipwrights of that name living in Lowestoft in the sixteenth century for the death of a Wyllyam Barnard, shipwright, is recorded in January 1580 in the Lowestoft records. His son Henry, born 1577, followed his father into the trade and his apprenticeship indenture, dated 17 May 1591, for a period of nine years, has survived (Appendix I). Other members of this family became shipwrights but they disappear from the Lowestoft records in the 1630s. However, at about the same time, a branch of the same family has been identified in the coastal town of Southwold, approximately twelve miles south of Lowestoft and 25 miles north of Ipswich. Some 60 years later a family of shipbuilding Barnards appear in the records of the ancient Borough of Ipswich itself and it is this branch of the family which is the subject of this work. No link has yet been established between the Lowestoft and Ipswich families (Appendix II).

The Borough of Ipswich, where this story begins, was granted its first Charter by King John in the year 1200. Its importance was due to its geographical location at the confluence of the River Gipping and the tidal waters of the River Orwell in a sheltered position some twelve miles inland from the North Sea. Throughout its long life the town experienced periods of great prosperity interspersed with periods of decline, mostly due to circumstances beyond its control. The first quarter of the eighteenth century saw the town in the grip of recession. The words of Sir Thomas Thornhill portray a dismal state of affairs when he wrote in 1711 of 'A town without people, a river without water and streets without names' [(2)].

The lack of water was the result of the silting-up of the Orwell, a state of affairs which had commenced in the seventeenth century and which, by the mid eighteenth century made it impossible for vessels of any size to use the Ipswich quays. Such vessels were forced to load and unload their cargoes into lighters at the so-called Downham Bridge, a natural underwater barrier some three miles downstream of the town.

The Barnard family of shipbuilders were resident in the Borough of Ipswich for a period of at least 87 years, their home being in the waterside hamlet of Wix Bishop in the parish of St Clements. The first recorded presence of the family is an entry in the 'Book of Admissions' of the Dissenters' Chapel in Tacket Street, Ipswich, which shows that on 4 August 1697 John Bernard (sic) was admitted as a member of the church [(3)].

John Barnard the Elder is a figure of shadow rather than substance, for little evidence has survived on which to build a picture of his life. His place of birth, for instance, has not been established while the year in which he was born can only be estimated from a possibly suspect source which gives the age at which he died as 52 years. If correct, that would make the year of his birth 1665 (Appendix III). He married, at some unspecified place and date, a woman named Mary, who may have been the widow of a man called Langley if a marginal entry in the aforementioned 'Book of Admissions' has been correctly interpreted. Both were members of a local sect of Dissenters and a son, John, was born to the couple in 1705. John Barnard the Elder was a man of some standing in the community as is confirmed by an entry in the Great Court Book of the Borough of Ipswich, which recorded that on 25 September 1711 he was admitted a Freeman of the Borough on payment of five pounds [(4)]. The first indication that he was a shipwright and shipbuilder is the appearance of his name and that of his wife Mary in an indenture, dated 20 September 1707, in which the couple were conveying to a Harriet Caston, a property including a shipyard, in St Clement's Parish. John Barnard is described in the indenture as "of Ipswich, in the County of Suffolk, Shipwright" [(5)]. Three years later, in 1710, the Land Tax Assessments for the hamlet of Wix Bishop [(6)] showed that he held a dockyard assessed at two pounds per annum. He died in 1717 (new calendar) and his will, dated 25 December 1716 (Appendix IV), commenced with the words 'I John Barnard....being sick and weak in body but of sound disposing mind and memory' bequeathed to his wife Mary a dockyard containing 'a Wharf, launch, key, dock and all other appurtenances thereby belonging' which he had lately purchased from Thomason Bloomfield and Mary Hubbard, executors of a Mr

Hubbard, who seemingly had been the owner of the most substantial yard in the parish [7].

The St Clement's shipyards were located at the south-eastern extremity of Ipswich at the point where the River Orwell takes a right-angle turn to the south. They are clearly delineated in the early maps of John Speed (1610), John Ogilby (1674), Buck brothers (1741) and Joseph Pennington (1778); the last named featuring Mr Barnard's house and extensive grounds. The area is

Ipswich 1778 showing the Barnard shipyards, house and garden (*Ipswich Borough Council Museums and Galleries*)

Detail from the Buck Bros print of 1741 titled 'The South West prospect of Ipswich in the County of Suffolk' showing the Barnard Shipyard in the Parish of St Clements. An original print is in the posession of the author. (*Ipswich Borough Council Museums and Galleries*)

Mr John Barnard the Younger
c. 1705 - 1784

now within the confines of the Wet Dock, formally opened in 1842.

At the date of her husband's death, Mary would have been some 50 years of age, with her only son John about to enter into his shipwright's apprenticeship with Edmund Gooday [8]. There are no records concerning Mary's management of affairs immediately following John the Elder's death but in all probability the day-to-day business would have been conducted by a competent foreman until such time as her son John could take over. There was certainly nothing unusual in that period in a capable woman taking over the running of a business on the death of her husband. John the Younger, even as an apprentice, would doubtless have played an ever-increasing role in the affairs of the yard. In this context it is interesting to note that, in accordance with an ancient Ipswich custom, a boy on reaching the age of twelve years, was considered to have come of age in respect of the ownership of property; subject only to his being able to do certain simple arithmetical calculations.

There is insufficient evidence to establish the extent and exact location of the Barnard property holdings in the parish of St Clements at any particular moment of time. For instance, a clause in an indenture of 1728, between an Arthur Barnardiston (no relation) and Edward Goody, suggested that at some date Mary had disposed of a dockyard in the said parish. The relevant clause describes it as ..'all that Yard, Key, and Dock, late in the possession of Mary Barnard, widow....' [9]. How this transaction fits into the overall picture of the Barnard presence in St Clements it is impossible to gauge but whatever the situation the foundations had been laid for the son John the Younger to build a successful business both as a shipbuilder and as a timber merchant. Mary died in March 1734.

Chapter II

John Barnard The Younger c.1705-1784

Shipbuilding on the Upper Orwell 1739-1742

John Barnard the Elder may well have laid the foundation for the Barnard family's rise to distinction in the field of shipbuilding, but it was his son, John the Younger, who changed the nature of the business from that of a relatively unimportant country yard, catering for local needs, to an enterprise building extensively for the Navy Board. He was born in the year 1705, but the place and exact date of his birth have not been established [10]. Little is known of his early life other than that in 1723 he was apprenticed to Edmund Gooday, a shipbuilder and Burger of the Borough of Ipswich; John would then have been about 18 years of age and probably in the last years of his apprenticeship. His letters, written later in life, show that he received a basic education obtained possibly at the Ipswich Academy for Dissenters, which was founded in the late seventeenth century by the Rev John Langston MA, pastor to the Ipswich sect of Dissenters. Upon completion of his apprenticeship John took over the management of the St Clement's Yard.

The earliest references to his activities as a shipbuilder concern not the building of ships but the building of a new Dissenters' Chapel in Tacket Street Ipswich. These references are to be found on a memorial to Mrs Deborah Conder in the burial ground of the Tacket St Chapel and also in a document written in 1894 by Thomas Conder, (a great, great grandson of John the Elder), entitled 'The Recollections of a Deacon', in which he claims that in 1721 John the Younger, with workmen from his shipyard, played a significant role in the building of the said Chapel. The story has been accepted at its face value and has appeared unchallenged in a number of local publications [11]. Not being central to this history it is dealt with in Appendix V.

John, at 23 years of age, in 1728 married Anne Notcutt, the daughter of the Rev William Notcutt, minister of the Dissenters' Chapel in Tacket St Their union produced eight children, three boys and five girls, the first born, John, dying shortly after birth.

In the year of his mother's death, 1734, John Barnard is recorded in the St Clement's Churchwarden's Rate Book [12] as the occupier of a 'Dock and yard in the Hamblet (sic) of Wix Bishop'. He had by 1739 established himself as one of the leading shipbuilders on the Upper Orwell: a position with which he might well have been satisfied had not the tide of history imperceptibly and irresistibly turned in favour of the merchant builder, for from that date on, the private builder was to play an ever increasing role in building ships for the Navy Board. It was also the first year in which details of a vessel built by the Barnard family appear in the records.

The said vessel, built to the specification of a Col Fuller was probably designed as a life-boat. The account of her launch, which in retrospect had its comic as well as its unfortunate aspects, was recorded in the Ipswich Journal of 29 September 1739:

"Yesterday a Boat of about Three Tons Burthen, of a new Design built by Mr Barnard according to the Direction of Col. Fuller, was hoisted by Slings off a Wharf near the *Falcon*, in the Presence of the Right Hon. Lords of the Admiralty, the Commissioners of the Navy and many other Gentlemen curious and skilled in the Art of Navigation. She is built in so particular a Manner that she cannot sink, tho' full of Water; But there not being Depth of Water enough, she struck upon a Pile, and stove a Hole in her Bottom: whereby the whole Design was defeated."

Table I
Naval vessels built on the River Orwell 1739-1742

Name	Rate	Guns	BM	Ordered	Launched
Biddeford	6th	20	433	14.10.1739	15.6.1740
Hampshire	4th	50	854	28.4.1740	13.11.1741
Granado	Bomb		279	14.9.1741	22.6.1742

This unfortunate fiasco must have been a great disappointment to both the designer and the builder; but with regard to the latter it should be noted that the vessel was not launched from his yard so that the disaster caused by the offending pile could not be placed at his door. It has been suggested that the presence of the 'Right Hon Lords of the Admiralty', together with the Commissioners of the Navy, had a bearing on the invitation to John Barnard to tender for a 20 gun frigate in mid-October 1739; but the relevant Admiralty orders show that the contract was but one of a bulk-order for frigates put out to tender to merchant builders at that time.

This sudden requirement for frigates, together with other vessels of war, arose as a result of the deterioration of Britain's relationship with Spain, which had been brought about by a number of different factors, the most controversial being the Spanish insistence on rigorously enforcing the rights, granted her by the Treaty of Utrecht, to stop and search any vessel suspected of breaking the restriction on foreign trade with Spain's Caribbean possessions as laid down in the said Treaty. For her part, Britain had the right to trans-ship, 5,000 slaves per annum and the cargo of one commercial vessel. Unfortunately the demand for slaves and British goods greatly exceeded the permitted quota, a state of affairs which led to large scale smuggling by the British merchants and in consequence to an increase in the stop and search activity by the Spaniards - a practice to which the British merchants took great exception. Co-existing with this maritime confrontation was a belief that war with Spain would bring rich pickings from the plunder of her Caribbean sources of wealth. The capture of her

A panoramic view of Ipswich showing the St Clements yard, left centre, with the frigate *Biddeford* on the stocks: c 1739 John Clevely
(*Ipswich Borough Council Museums and Galleries*)

treasure ships fostered such phantasies. The dispute intensified and became politicised, the Parliamentary opposition at Westminster whipping anti-Spanish sentiment to fever-heat. The well-publicised episode in which Capt Richard Jenkins startled a House of Commons Committee by producing a pickled ear which, he claimed, had been struck from his head by a Spanish stop and search party, exemplifies the mood of the times. Subsidiary disputes, including Britain's refusal to abandon Gibraltar, helped poison the relationship between the countries, and in October 1739 Britain declared war. The announcement was treated with acclaim by a largely ill-informed public and church bells were rung in celebration. Sir Horace Walpole, who opposed the war, is reported to have exclaimed "They are ringing the bells now but soon they will be wringing their hands". The so called War

of Jenkins' Ear would in time merge with that wider European conflict subsequently named the War of the Austrian Succession.

The fact that in 1739 the British fleet outnumbered the combined naval forces of Spain and France produced in the British public a false sense of overwhelming superiority and a frame of mind which overlooked the problems facing a fleet which had seen little active service since the turn of the century and the fact that both Spain and France had made increasing use of privateers in their use of naval power. Furthermore, with the threat of invasion of the U.K. ever present and the real possibility of an attack on Gibraltar, the Navy was ill equipped to embark on a hazardous venture some 4,000 miles across the Atlantic Ocean, especially in a theatre where, relatively, it had only a nominal presence and a complete lack of the

Location map of Suffolk shipyards

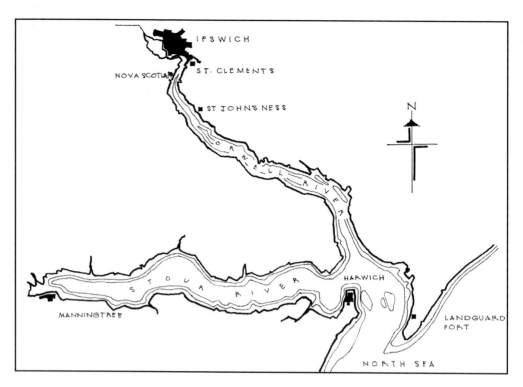

dockyard facilities vital for the repair, cleaning and victualling of vessels operating far from their home bases. Belatedly, action was taken by the Government to replace unserviceable vessels and to build additional tonnage. As part of the building programme initiated by the Admiralty in October 1739 orders were placed with merchant builders for a number of frigates. John Barnard received a contract for the *Biddeford*.

The Admiralty orders in respect of the tenders to merchant builders make interesting reading in that the five vessels named for replacement had been built in the Royal Dockyards as far back as 1711 and 1712.

4th Oct. 1739	"*Portmahon, Rose, Biddeford, Scarborough, Success.* To contract with Merchant Yards to build five 20 gun ships in their room"
8th Oct. 1739	"Not to contain ourselves to the building of the five 20 gun ships on the River Thames but to contract building them at such other places as we shall judge proper" [13].

A Navy Office minute of 1 November 1739 reveals that at that date there were at least eleven 20-gun ships under construction in merchant yards, the bulk of the contracts, nine in number, being placed with the merchant yards on the River Thames and only two with country builders, one of which, as stated above, was to John Barnard of Ipswich. The *Biddeford* was a frigate of 433 tons costing some £3750, plus rigging. The keel was laid 6 November 1739 in the St Clement's Yard and she was launched on 15th June 1740, two

weeks earlier than required by contract. On the 30 June she was towed downstream to the King's Yard, Harwich, to be rigged.

The 1733 Establishment 20-gun frigates were capable of being propelled by oars, the 36 oar-ports being located on the lower deck below the gun-ports.

A communication from the Admiralty to the Navy Board, made later in the same year [14], stated that complaints had been received concerning the standard of workmanship found in a number of the 20-gun ships built in the merchant yards. Lord Forrester, appointed to the *Biddeford* on 24 September 1740 claimed that 'she wanted new caulking before being fit for service'.

In its comments on the matter the Admiralty made the observation that it was:

"much surprised at those ships being so slightly put out of the contractors hands and the more so as a person was appointed by you (the Navy Board) to oversee the building and well fitting of our ships."

A strict enquiry was ordered, but no merchant builder appears to have been admonished. The overseer appointed by the Navy Board to supervise the said "building and well fitting" of the ship was usually a senior shipwright from one of His Majesty's Yards and was appointed immediately following the signing of the contract. The overseer in the case of the *Biddeford* was Thomas Slade, a man of outstanding ability who, in a relatively short passage of time, became Surveyor of the Navy. An appointment he held with great distinction. He was largely responsible for the development in this country of the 74-gun ship as well as designing Nelson's *Victory*. He died in 1771 as Sir Thomas Slade.

A letter from Thomas Slade to the Navy Board, written the day following the dispatch of the *Biddeford* to Harwich for rigging, has survived. It reads:

To the Honourable Principal Officers and Commissioners of His Majesty's Navy

"Honourable Sirs,

I most humbly acquaint your Honours that His Majesty's Ship *Biddeford* has been safely delivered into the charge of Captain Alline and that yesterday she was transported to Harwich.

I am, honourable Sirs,
Your Honours most dutiful and very humble servant
Thomas Slade

Harwich 1st July 1740" [15].

Harwich is situated some twelve miles downstream of Ipswich at the confluence of the Orwell and Stour Estuaries.

The previously-mentioned pressure on the Navy Board for additional tonnage continued unabated, and on 28 April 1740 the Admiralty issued the following order:

"*Hampshire, Nonsuch, Sutherland, Leopard.* To build four 50 gun ships in Merchant Yards of the dimensions of the *Gloucester*, viz 1733, in their room" [16].

Of the four named vessels the *Nonsuch* and *Hampshire* had been built by Thames based merchant builders in the years 1696 and 1698 respectively. The *Leopard* and *Sutherland* were built in 1703 and 1704 respectively, the former again being built on the Thames by a merchant builder and the latter in the Royal Dockyard at Deptford.

The contract for the *Hampshire* was placed with John Barnard of Ipswich, making it the second order for a naval vessel to be received by him within the space of some seven months. Other merchant builders also benefited from the increased activity. It is of special interest that Barnard was the only shipbuilder outside the confines of the River Thames to receive a contract from this programme. In the period 1733-40 twelve of these 50-gun ships were constructed, of which only the above mentioned four were contracted to merchant yards, the remainder being built in the Royal Dockyards.

In making a tender for the *Hampshire*, Barnard was faced with the problem of finding a suitable building site. The *Hampshire*, a ship of 50-guns and 854 bm, was approximately twice the size of the *Biddeford*. The St Clement's Yard was unsuitable for a vessel of her dimensions. His solution was to build her at John's Ness, a small yard about two miles down-stream from St Clement's. It was not a permanent shipbuilding site, but the configuration of the ground and the depth of water were eminently suitable for the task in hand. The site was duly approved by Thomas Slade.

It will be recalled that the *Biddeford* was launched from St Clement's on 15 June 1740 and that the *Hampshire* was ordered at the end of April 1740. Following the placing of the order for the *Hampshire* certain parties suggested to the Navy Board that John's Ness was an unsuitable site on which to build, launch and transport a vessel of the size of the *Hampshire*. The doubts raised caused Sir Jacob Ackworth, Surveyor to the Navy, to write to Thomas Slade demanding an explanation. Sir Jacob's letter has not survived, but Barnard's letter to the Board answering the allegations make the content of Sir Jacob's letter abundantly clear.

Dated 14 July 1740 [17], Barnard's letter was firm and very much to the point. He wrote that, having been shown the letter by Mr Slade, "he was very much surprised that any new difficulty should be started about the place which by Mr Slade's own opinion was thought both a convenient and safe place to launch and carry down the *Hampshire* or a 70-gun ship if required." He went on to say that "I have since consulted most of the ablest Pilots and old experienced Masters who all agree to a man 'tis easy and safe to carry down a ship of that Draft of Water without difficulty or hazzard." He buttressed his argument by stating that "being at the place designed to launch her (there is) not less than 14ft of water at low water and a sufficient length and breadth for the ship to be moored and at high water at spring tide not less than 24 or 25 feet of water." He assured the Board that in his opinion no damage would accrue during the building, launching or in carrying her down to Harwich to be rigged. His arguments must have carried the day, for there is no further correspondence on the matter and building proceeded as planned.

During the building of the *Hampshire*, letters from Barnard to the Navy Board refer to a number of matters which are of particular interest in that they disclose the diversity of problems which could arise between a builder and the Board. For instance, in a letter dated 21 February 1741 [18], the question of protection for shipwrights working on naval vessels against the activities of the press gang makes its first appearance in this correspondence. Shipwrights working on naval vessels in merchant yards were given certificates of protection which were probably the most valuable possession a working man could have, for they certified that the holder was classified as belonging to a reserved occupation. In this case, Barnard assured the Board that he had "granted Protection to none but such as are immediately employed in the service of his Majesty's Ship and shall comply with Your Honours orders in calling in Protections and numbering them and giving Mr Slade an account of same." From this it would appear that a merchant builder had the right to issue certificate of protection to those shipwrights working on naval vessels in his yard. It would also appear that the system was open to abuse, hence the Board's need for assurance.

Another matter of interest concerning his labour force comes to the fore in Barnard's letter of 18 March 1741, in which he thanked the 'Hon Members' for kindly interposing on his behalf in respect of two shipwrights who had deserted his yard for another merchant shipbuilder. Their Lordships had evidently ordered the other shipbuilder, a Mr Goody [19], either to return them to Barnard or discharge them. Barnard, whilst fully appreciating the Board's good intentions, preferred to leave the men where they were on the grounds that "men forced against their own inclinations will rather hinder than forward their work". He also observed, with pleasure, "that the affair had a salutary effect on the remainder of his workforce."

Other letters in this period disclose that Barnard, alongside his shipbuilding business, was a timber merchant of some standing. In May 1741 he wrote informing the Board that he had "a parcel of very good long timber in Suffolk that I am willing to sell for His Majesty's service if Your Honours please send some person to view some." In another letter, in which he was again offering timber, he concluded with the words "hoping to have the opportunity of converting it to His Majesty's service in another ship" [20].

On 31 October 1741 Barnard informed the Board that "God willing", and with the Board's consent, he intended to launch the *Hampshire* on either 12 or 13 November next. However, five days prior to the intended launch date, Barnard wrote to the Board expressing his concern at the non-delivery of certain ships stores, essential to the Pilot for the launching operation. His letter read:

"Honourable Sirs,

The *Hampshire* transport being safe arrived at Harwich yesterday, I examined the bill of lading and find she has on board no anchors nor cables fit for mooring or transporting His Majesty's Ship *Hampshire*. Humbly pray your Honours to order by tenders coming down with the men three anchors of ten hundredweight each, and two anchors of six hundredweight each, and three cables of ten inches each and two cables of seven inches each. These being the anchors and cables proper for the purpose. Honourable Sirs, I would have wrote sooner, but Mr Slade informed me Your Honours had ordered proper anchors and cables on board the ship and your pilot not being at home I could not tell what to write for. Beg Your Honours would hasten them down, we having no anchors proper to hold the ship when launched.

I am, Honourable Sirs, Your Honour's most dutiful obedient servant

John Barnard
Ipswich November the 7, 1741" [21].

The missing equipment did not, in fact, arrive as requested; nevertheless, on the intended day, 13 November, the *Hampshire* was launched. Barnard's letter to the Board of 14 November confirming the success of the operation explained that 'having no anchors or cables to bring her up by and moor her with, we did not break her loose'. Bad weather then intervened, and it was eleven days before she could be transported to Harwich for rigging.

The *Granado*, bombship

On 2 September 1741, Barnard tendered for a 44-gun ship at ten pounds ten shillings per ton and also for a 24-gun ship at nine pounds per ton; both tenders were unsuccessful. He did, however, succeed in securing a contract for the bombship *Granado* [22]. It was the only one of a batch of six bombships ordered at that time which was not built on the River Thames.

The bombship was a comparatively new addition to the fire power of the fleet. The principle on which it was based having been first tested by the French in the Mediterranean in the early 1680's, where it proved an outstanding success. Its purpose was to act as a sea-going siege-gun against land targets, and it was built to carry heavy mortars.

The *Granado* was ordered on 14 September 1741. The keel was laid on 18 November 1741, four days after the launch of the *Hampshire*. Her building site is uncertain, but as the Ipswich Journal referred to her 'having been built in the town' it is generally accepted that she was built in the St Clement's Yard. Her original armament was eight 4 pounder carriage guns, twelve half-pound swivel guns and two large sea mortars. She was launched on 22 June 1742 and was the last naval vessel to be built by Barnard on the upper reaches of the Orwell. Thomas Slade was again the overseer.

As a matter of peripheral interest the marine artist John Cleveley (1712-77) painted a composite picture of the three vessels, the *Biddeford*, *Hampshire* and *Granado* against a background of John's Ness, with the town of Ipswich in the distant background (see end papers). It is not known for whom the picture was commissioned, but John Barnard would seem to be the most likely candidate.

Chapter III

The King's Yard, Harwich, 1742-1748

The experience he had gained in his three years of contracting with the Navy Board showed John Barnard that if he continued to build only in the upper reaches of the Orwell his prospects of successfully tendering for larger vessels would be reduced to a minimum. Prompted, possibly by Thomas Slade, his thoughts turned to the King's Yard, Harwich, as an alternative building site which, as a naval building yard, had been on a care and maintenance basis since 1713. The yard had been established in the reign of Charles II and reached its peak of prosperity in the latter half of the seventeenth century.

The town of Harwich, an ancient sea port and country market town, is situated at the very tip of a narrow peninsula which thrusts north into the confluence of the Orwell and Stour estuaries. In 1739, at the outbreak of the War of Jenkins' Ear, the Navy Board had considered re-commissioning the yard [23] and a survey was duly carried out, but no action was taken. Thomas Slade was a member of the survey team [24]. In 1742, Barnard offered to build a 50-gun ship at a reasonable price if the Board would allow him to rent the King's Yard for its construction. After due consideration the Board gave its assent subject to having the right to repossess the yard should it so decide. Barnard, thereupon, took over the yard and Thomas Slade joined him as overseer [25].

The War of Jenkins' Ear had, by early 1742, merged with the War of the Austrian Succession. France had allied herself to Spain, and although a state of undeclared war had existed between Britain and France for a number of years, France did not formally declare war until 21 March 1744. For the most part mainly by the use of privateers, the French, concentrated their maritime efforts on attacking British shipping, both in home waters and on the high seas. Once again the Admiralty considered re-commissioning the Harwich yard and returning it to full establishment, but eventually decided that it would be more profitable to leave it in the capable hands of John Barnard. A tenancy which remained in being until the fateful year 1781.

The first vessel built by Barnard at the King's Yard was the *Harwich*, a 4th rate of 50 guns, which was launched 22 December 1743. Initially named the *Tiger* she was a replacement for a much rebuilt vessel of that name which had been wrecked in the West Indies in January 1742. Her name was changed from *Tiger* to *Harwich* just prior to her launch in recognition of the fact that she was the first naval vessel to be built in the King's Yard for some 48 years.

Further contracts followed for another three 50-gun ships of the same establishment in the years 1742-4. They were part of a building programme of fifteen similar vessels of which, all but one, were built in

Table II
Naval vessels built at Harwich 1742-1748

Name	Rate	Guns	BM	Ordered	Launched
Harwich	4th	50	976	21.8.1742	22.12.1743
Colchester	4th	50	976	6.9.1742	14.8.1744
Falcon	sloop	10	272	30.3.1744	12.11.1744
Eagle	4th	58	1130	10.4.1744	2.12.1745
Litchfield	4th	50	979	1.6.1744	26.6.1746
Severn	4th	50	1061	17.3.1746	10.7.1747
Seahorse	6th	24	519	4.2 1748	13.9.1748

Note: It is of interest that Nelson and Trowbridge, who became close friends, were midshipmen on the frigate *Seahorse* when she sailed for the East Indies in 1773; the *Seahorse*, which was an intermediate development in frigate design, had a long service life, being sold in 1784.

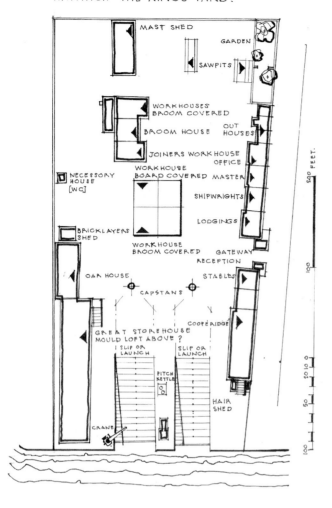

merchant yards. An analysis of the builders shows that Barnard, with contracts for four vessels, topped the list. Two other builders receiving contracts for two vessels apiece and the remainder receiving one per yard. Barnard also received a further contract for a 50-gun ship in 1746, but of a different establishment.

In principle the service lives of Barnard built ships will not generally be dealt with in these pages, except where circumstances are either out of the ordinary or are of particular historical importance. The circumstances surrounding the loss of the *Colchester* fall under the heading of the 'unusual' in that she was lost shortly after her launch and that the events which preceded her loss were bizarre in the extreme.

The Wreck of the *Colchester*

Nothing whatsoever is known of any day-to-day problems which may have beset the *Colchester* during her construction, for letters which may have been written to the Navy Board by Barnard in those years

have been lost. The first surviving letter for this period, written on 22 January 1745, revealed a disaster. The *Colchester* had been wrecked exactly two weeks after leaving her home waters [26].

The story of the events which preceded and succeeded her loss has been pieced together from a variety of sources including press reports, the log of her master (from the date of her launch until some ten days before the disaster), a letter from John Barnard to the Navy Board written following his visit to the wreck in January 1745, and the proceedings of the Courts Martial which automatically followed her loss [27].

Reference to Table II will show that she was launched on 14 August 1744. The next seven and a half weeks were spent in manning and rigging her, in taking aboard her armament and in storing and victualling her. At 2pm on Saturday 6 October, in moderate and cloudy weather, she slipped her Harwich moorings and sailed for the Nore. She arrived on Sunday 7 October. For the next week she lay at the Nore, lashed by gales interspersed by short periods of squally showers and low cloud [28].

The next to be heard of her was a report in the Ipswich Journal of Saturday 27 October 1744. It tells of her loss and the fears felt for the crew:

"Last Sunday Night about seven o'clock the *Colchester* Man-of-War, of 50 guns, which was lately built at Harwich, ran upon a Sand call'd the Kentish Knock, not far from the North Foreland. On Monday one of the Lieutenants came into Harwich in the Barge for Assistance, with about Ten or Twelve Men; upon which several Fishing Vessels went out directly: But the Wind being so high they could not get near the Ship, they return'd on Tuesday; and it was then apprehended that she would beat to Pieces the next Tide, and that there were no Hopes that any of her Men would be sav'd: However, some of the Fishing Vessels went out again that day.

The same Day, about Eleven o'clock in the Forenoon, the Surgeon and about Twenty-nine others came off in the Long Boat, who happen'd of a Collier, which took them aboard, and landed them at Lowestoft. They reported that the Ship was in so bad a condition when they left it that it must be destroy'd in a very short Time, and all the Men that were left will be inevitably lost.

But we have this Evening receiv'd the agreeable News, by a Letter from Harwich, that all the rest of the Men were taken out yesterday about Ten in the Morning and carried to the Nore, by the Harwich Fishing Vessels and Two Folkestone Cutters, except Two who were drowned endeavouring to get into the Boats, and about Ten men who were wash'd overboard at several Times. According to the last Account the Ship was lying on her side."

Her complement at the time would probably have been in the region of 350 men.

On 22 January 1745, some three months after the *Colchester* was wrecked, Barnard reported to the Navy Board his first sighting of the lost vessel:

"Honourable Sirs,   Harwich 22 Jan 1745

On Thursday the 17th inst. I sailed out of Harwich in order to save such stores as could be come at on board the wreck of His Majesty's Ship *Colchester*. I got to her by six o'clock in the evening, but found to my grief and surprise, at about half flood or less, the whole ship under water, only the end of her starboard cathead and the end of her bowsprit excepted. Nothing of any other part of the ship to be seen. I took the traveller off the stump of the flying jib boom. I found about 6, and from 6 to 8 foot of water around her, and very gradual shoaling on both sides of the sands. The ship lies on her larboard side, which is 10 feet under the sand, that I fear nothing can be got out of her. I would have gone sooner but had no opportunity, we having had so many gales of wind and such unsettled weather.

I am, Honourable Sirs, Your Honour's most dutiful and Humble Servant."

Endorsed Read 22nd[29]

The facts so far related would naturally lead to the belief that the *Colchester* ran aground and was lost in a violent storm. Nothing could be further from the truth. Her loss occurred solely as a result of pilot error whilst he was seeking a safe anchorage for the night. She, in fact, became stranded in light winds, in good visibility and in sight of land. At the time she was acting as escort to a merchantman laden with ordnance stores on passage from the Nore to the Downs. The Courts Martial, held at the Nore on 6 November 1744 aboard the *Royal Sovereign*, heard witness after witness testify that the pilot, John Benger, committed one of the most serious errors possible in that he had completely miscalculated the *Colchester's* true position.

The chronicle of her voyage, as gleaned from the evidence of the witnesses at the Courts Martial, shows that the *Colchester* left her mooring at the Nore at approximately 07.30hrs on Saturday 20 October 1744 and with the merchantman, the *Anne Jane*, in her care, sailed for the Downs. Both ships anchored for the night on the North Foreland Flats in thirteen fathoms.

At about 18.30hrs, the following evening, in the gathering gloom, the pilot gave the order to stream the buoy in preparation for dropping anchor for the night. So certain was he that he was in safe waters that he refused to sanction the frequent use of the lead although advised by fellow members of the crew. Even after the vessel first 'touched' he persisted in running on, insisting that he knew of 'no sand hereabouts'. His action resulted in the *Colchester* driving further on to a sand-bank, where, after grounding a number of times, she became stranded with her back broken. The storms which were shortly to break hastened her destruction.

The findings of the Courts Martial were that Capt Fredrick Cornwall had done his utmost to preserve the safety of His Majesty's Ship and was absolved of all blame, but that the pilot, John Benger, through his presumption and carelessness caused her loss. He was thereupon sentenced to two years imprisonment in the Marshalsea Gaol.

Perhaps the most damning piece of evidence against the pilot came from his own lips; for when asked by Henry Davis, mast-master, why there was no man in the chains using the lead, he answered, "it is no matter heaving so often. I see land, don't you think I know where I am."

The *Eagle*

In April 1744 Barnard contracted to build the *Centurion*, a 4th rate of 58 guns. She was the last 58-gun ship ordered. The Navy Board then upgrading the 1745 Establishment to 60 guns. Shortly before her launch, for reasons which are not apparent, she was renamed the *Eagle*.

From October 1748 onwards there are a number of letters from Barnard to the Board, which, although dealing mostly with routine matters concerning the *Eagle* do help unveil the complexities of shipbuilding in the eighteenth century, in this case in connection with the delivery of ships' stores and other such items. The collection and delivery of ships' stores between a country merchant builder and a Royal Dockyard posed a perpetual problem; the great number and weight of stores to be trans-shipped, coupled with poor means of communication, were the main difficulties faced by the parties involved. The fact that all dealings between the builder and the Royal Yards had to be conducted through the medium of the Navy Board did not help matters. In such circumstances the further a merchant yard was from a Royal Dockyard the greater the problems likely to arise. Barnard was obviously acutely aware of the difficulties and from the very early days employed his own vessels, (firstly he mentions sloops and latterly a brig) to fetch and carry stores, thus relieving the Navy Board of all responsibilities in respect of their transportation. However, arrangements did not always proceed according to plan, for on the 14 November 1745 Barnard wrote complaining that stores for the launch of the *Centurion*, which "God willing and with the approbation of Your Honours, will be on 29 November" were not ready for collection at Chatham when his sloops arrived [30]. Two days later, having received news that the sloops with the stores aboard were ready to sail, he wrote "humbly pray Your Honours would move the Right Honourable Lord Commissioners of the Admiralty, that a convoy may be speedily ordered for them" [31]. The sloops duly arrived in Harwich on 27 November carrying the bowsprit, mizzen mast, yards, topmasts, sails and other stores. On the day of the intended launch strong contrary winds upset high water predictions and the launch had to be delayed until Monday 2 December 1745 [32].

It is a matter of general interest that Captain James Cook (1728-79), the renowned navigator and explorer, was drafted to the *Eagle* in 1755 as an able-seaman, a position he held for only a short time, for due to his outstanding qualities he was quickly promoted to the warrant rank of boatswain. His later exploits are part of this country's history.

In the first week of May 1745 His Majesty George II, in his yacht *Caroline*, together with a number of men-of-war, was storm-bound in the Orwell estuary. Barnard paid a visit to the King's yacht on 7 May and reported that the King continued in good health. Mr Bagnold the overseer, who by this time had taken over from Thomas Slade, was not so fortunate: his attempt to reach the King's yacht was frustrated by bad weather [33].

A passing comment made by Barnard in a letter to the Board dated 23 May 1745 [34] once again draws attention to the prevalence of French privateers in home waters:

"We hear of a smart engagement between the *Falcon* and a French privateer and that the same privateer is taken and brought into Yarmouth Roads by His Majesty's Ship *Fox*."

The *Falcon* was a Barnard-built sloop of ten guns which, it will be recalled, was launched at Harwich 12 November 1744.

The Launch of the *Litchfield*

The launch of the *Litchfield* was a prime example of the sentiments expressed by Robert Burns when he wrote 'The best laid schemes o'mice an'men gang aft a-gley', for at 1 o'clock on the afternoon of 9 June 1764, as she slipped down her ways, the *Litchfield* lost momentum and slowly came to a standstill. Despite the valiant efforts of the launchmaster and his crew to move her she remained immobile. This most unhappy and potentially dangerous turn of events brought forth two letters to the Navy Board, one from Barnard and the other from the overseer Mr G. Bagnold. Barnard wrote:

"Honourable Sirs,   Harwich June the 10 1746
This come humbly to acquaint Your Honours that yesterday we launched His Majesty's Ship *Litchfield*, about a hundred and twenty feet, at which she stopped, being her whole length upon the launch. She sits very easy and safe, clear from the ground at least two foot and a half. We shall endeavour to heave her off this day; and I will give Your Honours the earliest account of her getting safe off. If not, shall beg the favour of the assistance of her officers and men with some blocks and falls proper for such purchases against the next spring.

I am, Honourable Sirs, in Duty Your Honours most obedient and most Humble servant.

John Barnard" [35].

Mr Bagnold's letter of the same date was in a similar vein, but stated that there was twelve and a half feet of water at the time of the launch, ample for the purpose, and suggested that the stoppage may have been caused by insufficient declivity in her ways.

After two days of fruitless effort Barnard wrote to the Navy Board requesting the attendance of 'some proper Officer that is acquainted with the nature of such work'. He also informed their Honours that 'She sits very fair upon her tallow without straining in any part' [36]. In answer to his plea a Mr Goodwin, Master Attendant of His Majesty's Yard, Deptford, and a Mr Pound, Builders Assistant, attended; but their efforts were without avail. They did, however, confirm that she was 'very well' and expressed the hope that they would heave her off at the next spring tide, an exercise which seemingly called for the use of a lighter for additional purchase. She was eventually successfully launched on the 26 June, but had missed the top of the tide due to the late arrival of the lighter [37].

Bagnold's letter to the Board reporting the launch was short and to the point and clearly expressed the feelings of all concerned; he wrote:

"This day was happily launched His Majesty's Ship *Litchfield* about 2 o'clock to the no small joy and satisfaction of Mr Barnard, as well as all the spectators" [38].

Barnard's "no small joy and satisfaction" must have known no bounds, for to have lost the ship could have doubtless cost him the patronage of the Navy Board. It is said that a week in politics is a long time; the seventeen days Barnard had to endure seeing one of His Majesty's ships perilously perched high on her ways must have seemed a veritable lifetime.

Her ill-starred launch was matched by a calamitous end for, by a stroke of bad luck, she ran aground and was wrecked on the Barbary coast at 6 o'clock in the morning on 29 November 1755. Under cover of darkness she had lost contact with a squadron bound for an attack on the French colony of Goree. At the time of her striking the ship's officers were under the impression that she was, at least, some 35 leagues distant from land. Lying with her broadside to windward, some two cables from a rugged shore, the heavy seas broke over her carrying her masts away and sweeping men with them. In spite of the heavy surf an attempt was made to launch a boat but it capsized with the loss of eight men. A makeshift raft was then constructed and a number of survivors struggled ashore where they were met by a large contingent of local Moors who treated them with the utmost barbarity being only interested in the loot they could strip from the living and the dead. By 1 December the *Litchfield* had completely broken up leaving two hundred and twenty survivors and one hundred and thirty drowned. The survivors, officers and men, were eventually marched to the city of Morocco where the Emperor obliged the men to work with his other Christian slaves. In April 1759 a sufficient ransom having been paid, the party was put aboard a ship at Sali bound for Gibraltar. The obligatory courts-martial which followed put the blame for the wreck on an uncertain current which had set the ship much further east than estimated.

Defence of The King's Yard, Harwich [39]

Throughout the year 1745 both Barnard and Slade were extremely concerned that the King's Yard would be attacked by French privateers, then active in the North Sea.

The yard was certainly a tempting target, for, isolated on a narrow peninsula, it had few defences other than the natural hazards of its approaches. The entrance to the Orwell and Stour estuaries was supposedly protected by Landguard Fort, some two miles across the waters on the Suffolk shore, but any defence the fort might have offered would have been ineffective against a determined raider. In 1745 the *Eagle* and the *Litchfield* were in an advanced stage of construction and would have been visible from the open sea. Voicing his fears, Barnard wrote to the Navy Board on 28 February 1745. The relevant paragraphs read:

"The occasions of my troubling Your Honours with these lines, is the sense of charge of His Majesty's Ships and stores here at Harwich, and how much we are exposed to the insults of the privateers, and how little we have to defend ourselves withall or to hinder an enemy from doing anything that their malice and covetousness may prompt them unto. I was surprised that when the prisoners came on shore from the privateer taken by the *Falcon*, that there were not arms in the whole town to equip 4 men in order to guard them till the Magistrate sent to me to borrow them. I humbly pray Your Honours would take our case into your consideration and will appoint such arms, with ammunition, as may at least put it in our power to act on the defensive part. If we had arms, we would endeavour to discipline ourselves, and cannons, we would fight them if occasion required; only one gun and one armourer."

The letter was read by the Board on 4 March 1745, but for reasons unknown no action was taken until 23 May 1745, when the Board brought the matter to the attention of the Right Honourable Lord Commissioners of the Admiralty. The outcome of the Board's approach was that at the end of May the officers at Deptford were ordered to fit out and dispatch to Harwich the hulk of the old *Winchester* (a 4th rate of 48 guns built by Wells of Rotherhithe in 1698) for the dual purposes of defence and for assisting in the task of careening ships' bottoms. Her complement was laid down as a boatswain, who would act as a gunner with two apprentices, a carpenter, also with two apprentices and 34 able-bodied seamen. The party was to be issued with forty muskets, twenty cutlasses and ten pairs of pistols. The storekeeper at Harwich and his staff were to be armed in a similar manner. Unfortunately the assembly of this small force appears to have taken an unseemly long time and, extraordinary though it may seem, Barnard does not appear to have been informed of what was afoot, for, on 27 August, nearly three months after the Admiralty instructions were issued, he made another appeal for help.

"The circumstances in which we are here on account of our being so very much exposed to the insults of the enemy, at this time the chief occasion of my troubling Your Honours; humbly praying that a suitable guard for the harbour and for His Majesty's Ships and stores here, may be the matter of Your Honours consideration. As Ostend is in the hands of the enemy and Landguard incapable of making any defense either for itself or for us and ourselves not able to act so much as in defense, not having one piece of cannon, pray Your Honours would be pleased to move the Right Honourable King's Commissioners of the Admiralty that some ship or ships may be ordered to guard and protect His Majesty's shipbuilding here (which are in great forwardness and may be seen at a long distance at sea) together with stores which are lodged in His Majesty's Yard and storehouse."

Even after this most reasonable plea he remained ignorant of the Admiralty's plans, for, on 17 October 1745, following the grounding of His Majesty's 60-gun *Dragon* on the Gunfleet Sands, which lie at the approaches to the estuary, he wrote and suggested that properly fitted out and manned with a hundred men (which he would provide) she would, if moved to the Rolling Grounds (off Landguard Fort) provide all the protection required. The suggestion was obviously ignored by the Admiralty in view of its own plans.

Six weeks later on 2 December 1745, just prior to the launch of the *Eagle*, the yard was still without protection, for Barnard wrote pointing out that his ships on the stocks 'are so near together one cannot be burned without the other'. Help did eventually arrive, for a month later on 2 January 1746 Barnard wrote, thanking Their Honours for the receipt of arms and ammunition. No further reference is made to the matter nor was the yard ever subjected to attack.

The *Seahorse* and the Harwich mail-packet [40]

The *Seahorse*, a frigate of 24 guns, was launched on 13 September 1748. Barnard had obtained the contract on 4 February 1748 by promising to complete the vessel in six months, which called for a delivery date in August of that year. Notwithstanding this commitment, he wrote on 11 July and requested a two month extension in order to build a mail-packet urgently required by the Post Office for the Harwich-Holland service, stating that the present packet was 'very leaky and bad'. The Board initially gave him permission to proceed, but then reversed the decision a day or two later, again demanding delivery of the *Seahorse* on the due date.

A two decker and a frigate running into Harwich, (Chas Brooking)

Barnard immediately responded by requesting the loan of eight or ten shipwrights in order to complete the vessel according to contract. He was, a few days later, to amend this request to four joiners and ten shipwrights, a request which was granted. The *Seahorse*, as stated above, was eventually launched on 13 September, just one spring tide later than the contracted date. The Navy Board did not demand a penalty for late delivery. Taken by and large the Board appears to have taken a very reasonable and relaxed stance throughout the whole episode. The fact that on 18 October the Peace of Aix-la-Chapelle was signed, bringing an end to the War of the Austrian Succession, may have been a contributing factor to the Board's attitude.

The Treaty of Aix-la-Chapelle had brought about a compromise cessation of hostilities to a war which, although European in origin, had spread across the globe as the imperial interests of the combatants came into conflict. Furthermore the final outcome was such that no side could claim victory, although Britain, by affirming her ascendancy over the combined naval forces of France and Spain, had learned lessons from which she would benefit in the battles to come.

On 21 December 1748, Barnard concluded this period of war-time building by writing to the Board as under:

"Honourable Sirs,   London December 21 1748
As building ships for His Majesty by contracting with Your Honours appears to be at an end by the concluding a good, and I hope, lasting peace, pray leave to propose to Your Honours to have His Majesty's Yard at Harwich for seven years at the rent of twenty pounds per annum, with a clause to leave it if wanted by His Majesty at half year's notice, to have the use of the yard and houses and mould loft as I now occupy there.

I am, Honourable Sirs, in Duty Your Honour's most Obedient and most humble servant

John Barnard" [41].

The Board agreed to the suggestion but required an increase in the rent to £30 per annum.

And so ended Barnard's first period of building for the Navy Board; a second period of intense activity would commence with the outbreak of the Seven Years War some eight years later in 1756.

Chapter IV

The King's Yard, Harwich, 1748-1763

An uneasy peace, 1748-56

The Treaty of Aix-la-Chapelle failed to settle the underlying differences between the warring Powers, especially between England and France, where the struggle for colonial supremacy in India, the West Indies and North America continued unabated. Eight years of uneasy peace ensued, followed by the outbreak of the Seven Years War, in 1756.

There is no evidence of the manner in which Barnard employed the facilities of the King's Yard during these years of peace. Correspondence with the Navy Board was reduced to a minimum, and only two letters have survived for the whole period. The first, written 13 July 1750, concerned payment for timber supplied, on contract, to the Royal Yard at Woolwich [42]. The second, dated 21 June 1751, was more unusual in that it referred to repairs required to some 'much decayed' fencing in part of the yard. The point at issue was whether Barnard or 'the King's Purse' should pay for the repairs. Although nothing further is known of the matter, the King's Purse probably had to settle the bill, as Barnard claimed that the fencing was in a poor state of repair when he had renewed the lease only two and a half years earlier [43].

The Nova Scotia Shipyard, Ipswich

Barnard must have been very confident that he could put both the St Clement's yard and the King's Yard to good and profitable use; for in 1749 he purchased, for the sum of £140, the freehold of a piece of land, including a shipyard and wharf amounting in all to about six acres, on the west bank of the Orwell some half mile south of Ipswich. He named the yard Nova Scotia [44]. The first recorded use of the yard by the Barnard family for the purpose of shipbuilding was in 1762-3 when Barnard's son William, in partnership with William Dudman, made use of the yard to build seven merchant vessels, including an East Indiaman. In the late 1770's, whilst still a tenant of the King's Yard, Barnard used the yard to build a number of sloops for the Navy Board. The West Bank Terminal now covers the site.

Just prior to the outbreak of the Seven Years War, Barnard entered into partnership with John Turner of Ipswich, who, it would appear, became responsible for the day-to-day conduct of the Harwich Yard. The style of the firm became 'Barnard and Turner'.

Table III
Naval vessels built at Harwich 1756-1764

Name	Rate	Guns	BM	Ordered	Launched
Mercury	6th	20	433	12.6.1755	2.3.1756
Achilles	4th	60	1234	14.11.1755	6.2.1757
Vestal	5th	32	659	25.5.1756	17.6.1757
Conqueror	3rd	70	1432	11.1.1757	24.5.1758
Alarm	5th	32	683	19.9.1757	19.9.1758
Terror	Bomb	10	301	21.9.1758	16.1.1759
Quebec	5th	32	685	16.7.1759	14.7.1760
Arrogant	3rd	74	1644	13.12.1758	22.1.1761
Druid	Sloop	10	212	19.8.1760	21.3.1761
Terrible	3rd	74	1644	13.1.1761	4.9.1762
Robust	3rd	74	1624	16.12.1761	25.10.1764

The Nova Scotia Shipyard 1782 (George Frost) (*Ipswich Borough Council Museums and Galleries*)

The Seven Years War, 1756-63

The years of peace were shattered when Frederick the Great attacked Austria in 1756, thereby lighting a fuse which led to a world-wide conflagration. William Pitt, with his intuitive appreciation of the situation, saw that supremacy at sea would bring eventual victory and laid his plans accordingly. His strategy was based on three considerations: firstly to contain the French army in Europe by supporting Frederick with men and money; secondly to neutralise French naval power by a tight blockade of French ports in Europe, and at the same time to cut off all French support for her colonies in the West Indies and North America; thirdly to carry the war to the French in Canada with a view to destroying her influence on the American continent.

Such a strategy could only succeed if the British Navy was of sufficient strength, equipped with vessels suited to their task, and was properly officered and manned. To meet the situation the Navy Board, both prior to and during the course of the war, placed orders for 56 ships-of-the-line, of which 30 were 3rd rates of 74 guns.

The number of Navy Board contracts received by John Barnard in these years exceeds that of any other period of his shipbuilding career. The *Arrogant*, shown in the following list, was the first 74-gun ship built by Barnard. She was also the first of her class to be built by a merchant builder outside the confines of the River Thames. Her designer was Thomas Slade. In order to encourage merchant builders to speed up the period of building, the Navy Board not only substantially reduced the time allowed but also offered cash inducements for early delivery. Such an inducement was included in the contract for the *Conqueror* which, dated 8 February 1757 [45], stipulated that at a cost of £16.5.0 per ton she should be launched in 24 months. The contract contained a further clause which offered

£16.7.6. per ton if launched in 21 months. To put the time factor into perspective, the usual time allowed by the Navy Board for a vessel of the *Conqueror's* size was in the region of 36-40 months.

Messrs Barnard and Turner accepted the challenge with alacrity and she was launched on 24 May 1758, only some fifteen months after the laying of her keel on 9 February 1757. Reference to the matter was contained in evidence given by Barnard to a Parliamentary Committee which sat in March 1771 to enquire into how His Majesty's Navy 'may be better supplied with timber' [46]. In answer to a question Barnard informed the Committee that 'in the last war he had built and launched a 70-gun ship within a year'. The ship was, of course, the *Conqueror*. It is not suggested that the haste with which she was constructed had any direct bearing on her subsequent history for she was certainly not a lucky ship. Disaster struck early, for on the day of her launch, her launch-master was crushed to death as she slid down her ways [47], and only some twenty-nine months later, on 26 October 1760, she was wrecked in Plymouth Sound whilst attempting to leave a temporary mooring on the south eastern tip of St.Nicholas Island (now Drake's Island) in order to move into the Royal Dockyard in Hamoaze for cleaning. Evidence given at the Courts Martial which followed show that her loss in inclement weather was due to a chapter of accidents most of which, with only a modicum of luck, could have been avoided. Her Captain and Master were absolved of all blame for her loss, but the pilot, one Henry Harris, was sentenced to eighteen months in jail 'for his lack of knowledge as a seaman' [48].

Three of the other ships in the above list, the *Alarm*, *Achilles* and *Quebec* also call for comment: the *Alarm* because she was the first naval vessel to be sheathed with copper in an attempt to overcome the ravages of the ship worm teredo; the *Achilles* on account of her successful two hour battle on 4 April 1759 with the French *Comte De Florentine* off Cape Finisterre, when the Frenchman struck his flag after being demasted and suffering heavy losses; the *Quebec*, as a result of her spectacular end, when she blew up following a duel with the French *Surveillante* off Ushant on 6 October 1779. Although heavily outgunned she had continued the battle even after eighty of her crewmen and her Commander, Capt Farmer, had been killed. She sank, taking with her most of those on board, a total of one hundred and fifty souls. George III conferred a baronetcy on Captain Farmer's son in recognition of his father's outstanding gallantry.

Unfortunately only two small batches of Barnard's letters to the Navy Board have survived for this period of intense activity, the first batch covering the six months prior to the launch of the *Achilles* [49] and the second covering the six months to the launch of the *Robust* [50]. In both instances the letters deal mostly with routine

3rd June 1762, *Alarm* conducting Spanish prize into Gibraltar (Carrington Bowles)

questions concerning the launch of the two vessels. Barnard's letter of the 17 November 1756 is a typical example of both the business and technical side of the launch of the *Achilles* and of the deferential but down-to-earth approach adopted by merchant builders in their dealings with the Navy Board:

London, November 17. 1756

"Honourable Sirs,
We being in such forwardness in the sixty-gun ship building at Harwich for His Majesty's service, that we are in need of the pumps, light for the store room, and other stores, and having a ship ready to sail for the same stores to Chatham, humbly offer the same ship to bring the said stores at the rate of ten shilling a ton as I have already had.
And being at need of a pair of bilgeways, there being a pair at Chatham, humbly pray your Honours will order the officer to put them on board our ship and I will take care and return them into store as soon as I have done with them.
And as we must lay some ground way to secure our launch, humbly pray your Honours would order some old timbers for the same, if there by any to spare.

I am, Honourable Gentlemen, in Duty Your Honours' most Humble Servant,
John Barnard
To the Honourable Commissioners of His Majesty's Navy."

A later letter reveals that the Navy Board had complied with Barnard's request for the bilgeways but that the pair supplied were for an 80-gun vessel, and therefore unsuitable for a ship of 60 guns. Barnard suggested that the "*Dunkirk's* bilgeways are at Woolwich and as she is the similar body to the ship at Harwich, I humbly pray your Honours would give an order to the Officer at Woolwich to deliver them..." A request which was seemingly granted.

On a more unusual note, Barnard, in a letter dated 25 December 1756, offered to trans-ship ship's stores from Woolwich to Hull in his own vessel, the *Speedwell*, for delivery to the frigate *Rose* building in Messrs Blayde's shipyard, his charge for the service being thirteen shillings and sixpence per ton. In view of the ever-present threat to coastal shipping posed by marauding French privateers, Barnard informed the Board that "the *Speedwell* is fitted both for offence and defence... she fighting ten guns close 3 pounds and well fitted for close quarters."

In the second batch of Barnard's letters to the Navy Board two points arise which are worthy of note, firstly that John Turner, writing on behalf of the partnership, pleaded for a supply of iron bolts which the Navy Board had been loath to supply:

Quebec (centre) engaged with *Surveillante*

Harwich,   4th September 1764
"Honourable Sirs,
We received Your Honours' favour of the 27th August, and
return Your Honours thanks for the grant vouchsafed to us
of the bilgeways and spurs for launching His Majesty's ship
Robust, but are extremely sorry that the bolts are refused,
being at their time greatly distressed both for want of
suitable iron for that service, and from a scarcity for the use
of bolts, with the bilgeways and spurs, will be excused by
Your Honours, as our present necessity obliges us to be
solicitous for them. Should Your Honours condescend to
grant us the favour, we would take particular care to return
them safe without diminution.

I am, honourable Sirs,
for Mr Barnard and self
Your most obedient humble servant,
John Turner."

The letter not only illustrates one of the problems of
the time but also that iron fastenings and the like were
fashioned on site in the smith's shop. There is no record
of the reply made by the Navy Board.

The other point worth recording in this batch of
letters concerns a request by the firm of Barnard and
Turner that the launch of the *Robust* be postponed for a
month due to unsatisfactory workmanship in respect
of the 'carved work'.

Two other events which occurred during the 1756-64
shipbuilding programme, whilst not relating directly to
the vessels built, are nevertheless important episodes
in the history of the Barnard family. They concern,
firstly, the arrival of Princess Charlotte of Mecklenburg
and secondly, the building of an East Indiaman by
William Barnard, son of John, at the Nova Scotia Yard.

Princess Charlotte of Mecklenburg

On 6 September 1761 Princess Charlotte, bride-to-be of
George III, arrived in Harwich after a tempestuous ten
day voyage from Cuxhaven. The Royal Yacht *Caroline*,
in company with other yachts, had been escorted by a
squadron of naval vessels commanded by Admiral
Lord Anson. The arrival was rated as a major event by
the media, 'the eager and anxious curiosity of the
people of England was never more conspicuous than
during the interval', wrote a spectator, and the event
was recorded by a number of the leading artists of the
day. John Barnard, as the Navy Board's tenant of the
yard, had the honour of acting as receiving host,
handing the Princess ashore and then escorting her
across the yard to her awaiting carriage. According to
John Barnard's grandson, Edward George Barnard, MP
for Greenwich 1832-51, John Barnard was offered a

Quebec blows up after engagement

knighthood for this small service, an offer he politely refused, saying that he would much prefer a contract for a new ship. As the contract for the *Robust* was dated 16 December 1761 the report could be authentic especially as at that date Barnard already had the *Terrible* of 74 guns building on the stocks.

There has come down through the years a delightful but probably fanciful story concerning the presentation by Barnard to the Princess of a basket of grapes grown in his greenhouse in the grounds of his residence in Ipswich. It is claimed that Princess Charlotte shared the grapes with her husband to be, George III, who, being impressed by their quality enquired from whence they came. On being informed that they were the product of the greenhouse of John Barnard, shipbuilder of Ipswich, he promptly requested a cutting which was duly supplied. The cutting, so the story goes, flourished until, as a full grown vine, it achieved national acclaim. At this point the sources from which the story is drawn diverge. On the one hand it is said that the vine was in the vinery at Kew Gardens, on the other hand, Hampton Court has been credited with its presence. Unfortunately an examination of the records of both establishments has failed to either confirm or deny the story. It would be satisfying to believe that

although embroidered with the passage of time, somewhere at the heart of this whimsical tale there is an element of truth [51].

The *Speaker*, East Indiaman

Although the *Speaker* was built in 1762-3 by William Barnard in partnership with William Dudman in the Nova Scotia Yard, part of the story of her building concerns John Barnard, and must, therefore, appear in this narrative. It is not known how the partnership acquired the contract, for very few East Indiamen were built outside the River Thames, but it may well be that Barnard Snr. had a hand in the matter. Should this be the case although his name did not appear in the contract, he took more than a passing interest in her construction. It was an interest which was to bring him into direct conflict with the Rev William Gordon, pastor of the Dissenters' Chapel, Tacket St, of which John Barnard was a leading member.

The contract for the *Speaker*, a vessel of 700 tons, stipulated that she was to be launched on the first spring tides of February 1763, with the usual penalty for late delivery and a bonus of £50 if launched in January. Building commenced 30 of July 1762, thereby giving the partnership some seven months to completion.

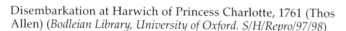

Her Majesty QUEEN CHARLOTTE landing at HARWICH.
on her way to St. James's Palace. Sep.r 7, 1761.

Disembarkation at Harwich of Princess Charlotte, 1761 (Thos Allen) (*Bodleian Library, University of Oxford. S/H/Repro/97/98*)

Rev. William Gordon D.D.

Rev William Gordon D.D.

Whether it was a father's natural interest to ensure that his son's first venture was a success or whether he privately had a financial stake in the enterprise will never be known, but whatever the reason he acted as if he were a principal in the matter rather than just an interested party. It may well be that his experience told him that only by keeping up an intense pressure on the workforce could the contract date be met. The intensity of his interest was noted by the Rev William Gordon, a zealous and dogmatic cleric, to whom the letter of the religious teaching, as he understood it, was sacrosanct. The Rev Gordon became convinced that the vessel could not be completed on time unless the men building her were instructed to work on the Lord's day, a thought totally abhorrent to a man with his principles. He first broached the matter to John Barnard one Sunday after morning service whilst they were having a quiet smoke together in the vestry. Barnard, irritated by the Rev Gordon's interference

brusquely brushed the matter aside as hypothetical. The Rev Gordon then took it upon himself to approach the Town Magistrates asking them to exert their power 'for the prevention of a needless prophanation (sic) of the Sabbath'. He found little support in that quarter. In a somewhat furtive manner he started visiting the yard, pleading with the shipwrights not to work on the Sabbath should they be so requested. His pleas received a mixed reception. John Barnard, although annoyed by the minister's unwelcome activities, continued to insist that it was most unlikely that Sunday working would be necessary. He was wrong. On Sunday 5 December the men were asked to report 'same as upon a common day'. Most of the workforce complied. The Rev Gordon bided his time, then in his New Year's sermon, (seemingly an oration locally considered of some importance), he launched from the pulpit a savage and scathing attack on Barnard for openly and deliberately defiling the Lord's Day. Later he was to write that he considered his outburst 'as a public testimony against public sin' but he also admitted that 'the sermon gave great offence and made much talk'. The affair did him little good; for a year later he quietly quit Ipswich for places unknown. He later appeared in North America supporting the colonists in the American War of Independence. It was locally believed that he was, for a time, secretary to George Washington, a claim not substantiated by the records [52].

The *Speaker* was launched on Monday 30 January 1763, thus allowing the £50 bonus to be claimed.

Later in the year the partners William Barnard and William Dudman took a lease of a yard on the River Thames where, in partnership with Henry Adams of Beaulieu, they established a shipbuilding enterprise.

The ending of the Seven Years War and the signing of the Peace of Paris on 10 February 1763 confirmed Britain's mastery of the seas; it also ensured that English, not French, would become the language of North America. William Pitt and his administrators had achieved an outstanding victory; but it was a victory which was to have a dark and unexpected side, for, to quote Winston Churchill:

"Little did he (Pitt) know that in so doing he would open the door to the secession of the North American Colonies."

Although it was not apparent at the time, by the removal of the French threat he also lessened the colonists' dependence on British arms, which, in turn, allowed them to adopt a more independent stance in their dealings with King George III and his ministers.

In the year 1766 John Barnard had the honour of being appointed High Sheriff of the County of Suffolk (Appendix VI).

Chapter V

The King's Yard, Harwich, 1763-1776

The North American Colonies

The inherent difference in outlook between King George III and his ministers in England and the thirteen North American Colonies led initially to friction, followed by armed rebellion, and finally to the Declaration of Independence in 1776.

A study of the shipbuilding programmes initiated by the Navy Board between the years 1763 and 1776 confirms that George III and his chosen ministers completely failed to anticipate the likely consequences of the stance they adopted in respect of taxation and other matters of concern to the Colonists. Although in England support for the war was by no means universal the King's party believed, almost to the very last, that the rebels could be subdued by force of arms, unfortunately the means by which such a victory might possibly be obtained were not forthcoming. For their part the rebels, or patriots in American terms, had their own serious internal problems but, with the support of a majority of the population, their armies eventually won the day. Muddled thinking at home and serious errors of strategy on the part of the British commanders were contributory factors in the final outcome. The Boston Tea Party, Lexington and Concord, the Battle of Bunker's Hill, the rallying cry 'No taxation without representation' and the Declaration of Independence have become shining beacons in American history - a history which shows that in the relatively short period of some 150 years the thirteen colonies, as the United States of America, grew to become one of the Great Powers of the 20th century.

In England the failure by the ruling party to appreciate the extent of the dangers inherent in a deteriorating situation is revealed in the sluggish reaction of the Government in respect of naval requirements. The number of ships of the line ordered between the years 1763-76 remaining at a low ebb. This lack of urgency is reflected in the fact that, following the Seven Years War, it was not until 1770 that the merchant builders were again requested to contract for naval vessels.

Navy Board 'In Letters'

Eleven partnership letters to the Navy Board for the years 1771-5 have survived, dealing mostly with launch dates, the loan of bilgeways, miscellaneous equipment and the availability and collection of ships-stores, in other words, matters common to the launch of any vessel [53]. On the other hand a letter of 23 March 1774, concerning the launch of the *Centurion*, raises the question of safety, the partnership suspecting that a sunken hulk, acting as a breakwater, might present an unacceptable hazard.

The relevant passage of the letter reads:

"We humbly beg leave to acquaint Your Honours that on examining the situation of the Argyle Breakwater lying near to His Majesty's yard at this place, appear to be in the direction of the launch of His Majesty's ship *Centurion*, from the stern timber to the foreside of the gallery door of the *Argyle*. It being our indispensable duty to lay the same before Your Honours previous to the launch, for Your Honours' consideration, and Your Honours' instructions therein shall be most carefully complied with" [54].

There is no record of any action being taken.

Two other letters must be recorded. The first, dated 3 October 1775, is a simple request that:

Table IV
Naval vessels built at Harwich 1770-1776

Name	Rate	Guns	BM	Ordered	Launched
Orpheus	5th	32	708	-	7.5.1774
Centurion	4th	50	1044	25.12.1770	27.5.1774
Sultan	3rd	74	1614	23.3.1771	23.12.1775
Cormorant	sloop	14	304	30.10.1775	21.5.1776

Facsimile of John Barnard's letter to the Navy Board apologising for the negligence of his partner, John Turner, in respect of the use of inferior trennels

"...the lease which I made with the Honourable Board in 1757 for His Majesty's Yard at Harwich is now expired, humbly pray the renewal of the same upon the same terms" [55].

Breach of Contract [56]

The second letter, dated 2 February 1775 is possibly the most serious written by a member of the Barnard family to the Navy Board. It concerned a complaint made by the Navy Board which could well have cost John Barnard his livelihood. However, before dealing with the matter it is necessary to note that the partnership between John Barnard and John Turner was dissolved by mutual consent in 1765, John Turner died 17 October 1771. His son John, at some unspecified date, was offered a partnership; it was a move which, in the course of time, Barnard would come to regret, for his new partner would prove more of a liability than an asset.

The Navy Board's complaint was in respect of an incident which occurred during the building of the *Sultan* and was one in which young John Turner played the leading role. The Navy Board minute of 5 February 1775 reveals the severity of the affair:

"Acquaint Mr Barnard with our disaprobation (sic) of Mr Turner's behaviour for attempting to use improper materials and insulting our Overseer, which demands the most severe censure."

The accusation of using materials in breach of contract was one of the most serious charges which could be levelled against a merchant builder; and then to compound this malpractice by insulting the Board's representative can only have added fuel to an already inflammatory situation. The Board asked for it to be noted that the incident would be remembered when contracting in the future. A potent threat indeed.

The matter was brought to light in January 1775 when Mr Hellyer, the Overseer, wrote to the Navy Board complaining that he had been ill treated by Mr Turner for objecting to work not being carried out according to the terms of contract. The Navy Board immediately instructed Mr Binmer, Assistant to the Surveyor of the Navy, to investigate and, at the same time, to stop any Navy Bills due - a punitive measure of major impact. Mr Binmer's report stated that, though there had been some skimping of material, the rest of the ship was satisfactory. It would appear that Barnard was unaware of what had occurred until advised by Mr Binmer; he then hastened to Harwich to make his own enquiries. His letter of explanation and apology to the Navy Board, dated 2 February 1775, may be summarised as follows: the trouble had arisen, he reported, when Mr Pike, a carpenter, drew the attention of the overseer, Mr Hellyer, to the use of trennels made of East Country oak (instead of English oak, as per contract), in part of the construction of the *Sultan*. Mr Hellyer, when reporting the matter to Mr Turner, obviously received a most abusive reply. When questioned by Barnard how he possibly could have been guilty of allowing such a breach of contract, Turner replied that he had merely ordered some ends of planks lying about the yard to be rove into trennels, adding that he could not tell whether it was East Country or English oak - a remarkable admission for a man with his responsibilities. Barnard's letter to the Board was tactful in the extreme and ended with the following:

"....Mr Hellyer's discovering them gave me pleasure, this I can with justice say of Mr Hellyer, he have been faithful to his duty and diligence in the execution of it, and his natural temper is kind and humane, but will see justice done to his trust....... I am very glad such discovery was made and prevented any such trennels or other materials not agreeable to contract going into the ship as I have always made it an act of honour and integrity to all my judgements with this Honourable Board."

HMS *Orpheus* 1780-7, 5th rate, 32g. frigate

Whether or not this incident adversely affected Barnard's personal standing with the Board it is impossible to say: he certainly continued to receive contracts for further vessels but it was many years before he received another contract for a 74-gun ship - a ship which, in fact, would prove to be the last he would build.

John Turner was again in trouble in December 1775 when Barnard had to ask the Navy Board to allow him to build the sloop *Cormorant* at the Nova Scotia Yard instead of Harwich ' by reasons of the stock which Mr Turner is not willing I shall meddle with' [57].

It is not surprising that the Barnard-Turner partnership was dissolved on 4 March 1776. John Turner was declared bankrupt on 6 July 1776.

Chapter VI

The King's Yard, Harwich, 1776-1783

Naval Building Programmes

The Declaration of Independence in 1776 forced the British Government to accept that it was engaged in a major conflict some 3000 miles across the Atlantic Ocean. Thrust into action orders were placed for 52 ships-of-the-line between the years 1776-82 of which only four were built in the Royal Dockyards.

The problems facing the Navy were many and varied for not only had it to protect the line of communication between Britain and America but also had to perform the same duty in respect of other British interests throughout the world. In the North American theatre it was expected to blockade 1000 miles of coastline and support the military in amphibious operations. In home waters sufficient strength had to be maintained to protect these islands from invasion.

Initially the naval force available on the North American station amounted to only some 30 vessels. By the end of 1776 it was increased to 70 vessels. Although the strength of the naval presence grew as the war progressed there were never sufficient vessels to deal with the situations which arose. The decision of France and then Spain to enter the conflict on the side of the colonials, together with the British declaration of war on the Dutch, in effect, put the final outcome of the war beyond doubt. On 17 October 1781, General Cornwallis, trapped at Yorktown by superior forces on land and blockaded by a French fleet dominating Chesapeake Bay, surrendered with seven thousand men.

The role played by John Barnard in the new building programme was in a somewhat minor key for between 1776 and 1778 he only contracted for seven naval vessels, two 3rd rates of 74 guns, a 3rd rate of 64 guns, a frigate, a 6th rate and two sloops. Furthermore only four of the vessels were built at Harwich, the Nova Scotia Yard and the hard at John's Ness being called into service.

Wreck of the *Proserpine*

The *Proserpine* came to an unhappy and unusual end. On 1 February 1799, bound for Cuxhaven, she was caught in a blizzard and ran aground on the Scharhorn Riff in the River Elbe. Ice built up around her and her timbers gave way under the pressure, her stern post was broken in two. The only escape route for the ship's company was to walk six miles across the ice to the island of Neuwerk. One hundred and eighty seven people set out; seven crewmen, four marines, a woman and child and a boy perished on the journey.

In all fifteen letters from Barnard to the Navy exist for this period, most of which deal with matters of routine, however, a small number concern matters either of special interest or concern issues not before dealt with in this correspondence. For instance, two letters, one dated 31 May 1776 and the other 27 August 1779 deal with matters of construction which, being part of the contract between the parties have not usually been subjects of discussion. The letter of 31

Table V
Naval vessels built at Harwich, Nova Scotia and John's Ness 1777-1782

Name	Rate	Guns	BM	Ordered	Launched	
Zebra	sloop	14	306	24.5.1776	8.4.1777	N.Scotia
Proserpine	6th	28	596	14.5.1776	7.7.1777	Harwich
Savage	sloop	14	302	12.3.1777	28.4.1778	N.Scotia
Charon	5th	44	891	9.10.1776	8.10.1778	Harwich
Champion	6th	24	519	11.2.1778	17.5.1779	John's N.
Inflexible	3rd	64	1386	5.2.1777	7.3.1780	Harwich
Irresistible	3rd	74	1643	5.2.1777	6.12.1782	Harwich

The ships company of the frigate *Proserpine* setting out on a six miles walk across the ice to Neuwark, an island in the river Elbe

May 1776 is a direct tender for a sloop to be built at Ipswich at a price of 'nine pound fifteen shillings a ton in nine months'. An endorsement on the letter by the Navy Board secretariat states that:

"Board's offer £9.10.0.
which Mr Barnard agreed to accept
The frame to be completed by the end of September next.
The thick stuff and beams to be prepared and completed by the end of October next.
The frame, thick stuff and knees to stand together to season till the end of January 1777.
The sloop to be completed and launched by the end of May 1777.
Under the penalty of £5 per ton in case of failure in any one of the above mentioned particulars.
This addition to the Minute of 31 May 1776 made by order of the Surveyor, 22 June 1776."

Subsequently the Board informed Barnard that they preferred the sloop to be built at Harwich rather than Ipswich, however after informing the Board that the *Cormorant* had been successfully launched from the Ipswich Yard, which was "a very safe and commodious place to build such ships in.....notwithstanding the tides were remarkably small". He further informed the Board that "as two different parcels of shipwrights will be severally employed, as they do not well agree together, I can carry-on the work much better."

He got his way, and the sloop, the *Zebra*, was duly launched on 8 April 1777 some five weeks before the contract date of delivery.

The letter of 27 August 1779 gives details of the work completed on the *Inflexible* when requesting payment of the seventh instalment, the penultimate before completion. The details were:

"I having on His Majesty's ship *Inflexible* wrought the sheerstrake and shut in under it, and have got in the upper deck beams and bound them, the decks framed, have wrought the binding strakes, waterways and spirketting, have provided and brought into the yard the strings of the waist, ship clamps for the quarterdeck and forecastle beams, with the quarterdeck, forecastle and roundhouse beams cut and trimming, and everything for the ship provided, humbly pray your Honours would order me a Bill for the seventh payment. The eighth I shall not ask for till the works are all complete. It will enable me to carry on the works with greater speed and spirit."

A letter on an entirely different subject was written on 26 June 1776. It was an impassioned plea to be excused the payment of a penalty for the late delivery of the *Cormorant*, a 6th rate launched on 21 May 1776. It read:

"Honoured Sirs,
I saw yesterday with surprise and concern the order from this Honourable Board to inflict the penalty of £100 on the account of the *Cormorant* not being launched according to the time of the contract, it being impossible for me to do it by reason of the hard weather we had for a month, and the rain that followed, that hindered us more than the time (I convey) beyond the time of launching, that if my life had been at stake I could not have built her sooner. Humbly pray your Honours would take it into consideration, as I have with honour served this Honourable Board above this forty years. I have at the desire of this Honourable Board launched several ships before the time, working night and day. Humbly pray your Honours would give direction that the penalty may be taken off.I am in Duty your Honour's most Humble Servant John Barnard."

The reply made by the Board is unrecorded.

Failure

The year 1781, was an unhappy one both for the nation and for the Barnard family for in the same year that Cornwallis surrendered at Yorktown, John Barnard, shipbuilder of Ipswich, had been declared bankrupt.

The first indication that anything was seriously amiss with his financial affairs was contained in a letter to the Navy Board from Mr Russell, the Naval Officer in charge of a small maintenance party at Harwich, which reported that on 12 February 1781 the artificers employed on the *Irresistible* had stopped work as Barnard "has neither the material to work with nor the money to pay the men their wages". The Board informed the Admiralty by letter on 15 February [58], and The London Gazette duly reported his failure [59]. Barnard was summoned to appear before the Commissioners of Bankruptcy meeting on 15 and 16 March at the Coffee House, Ipswich. Following the customary examination he was formally declared bankrupt. Assignees were appointed, one of whom was his son William, shipbuilder of Deptford.

Bankruptcy was no stranger to those engaged in the business of shipbuilding. Throughout the ages it had been a precarious occupation, the margin between success and failure being very finely drawn, a situation of which Barnard would have been well aware. Why then, after so many years of unqualified success, should disaster so suddenly strike? There appears to be no simple answer. The most feasible explanation being that it was caused by the accumulation of a number of adverse factors concentrated into a relatively short period of time.

One factor which may well have played a major part in his failure was the decision of the Navy Board in 1777 to replace the old established practice of making an initial payment to the builder upon the signing of the contract by one which withheld payment until the builder certified that he had sufficient timber on site to permit building to commence. Apart from the fact that the builder was obliged to finance the initial outgoing from his own cash resources and then claim these monies expended from the Admiralty, the question of the manner of payment had to be taken into account. The method of payment employed by the Navy Board was in the form of post-dated Navy Bills which were not easily negotiable and could only be encashed by the acceptance of large discounts. The keel of the *Irresistible* was laid in October 1778. Should the Navy Board's new direction have been enforced then, bearing in mind the prodigious amount of timber of various types required to build a 74-gun vessel, the cost of such timber could have played havoc with Barnard's cash resources. Barnard's statement from Alexander's Bank, Ipswich, shows that between 1778 and 1782 he was paying between $7\frac{1}{2}\%$ and $11\frac{1}{4}\%$ in order to obtain encashment of Navy Bills (Appendix VII). Even in stable conditions such rates would adversely effect profit margins; but with Britain not only at war with the newly formed United States of America but also with three of her European neighbours, conditions were ripe for the evils of inflation to exert their pressures.

The rises which occurred in the cost of food, raw materials and labour as a result of the war, were probably the main causes of Barnard's bankruptcy. It must be remembered that all contracts between the Navy Board and the merchant builders were at fixed prices, with no escape clause. Bearing in mind that a 3rd rate took at least some three years to complete, it will be seen that in certain conditions fixed price contracts were a recipe for disaster. Furthermore it would be logical to suppose that in such conditions the more work a shipbuilder had on hand the greater the risk of escalating losses. A series of such losses could quickly absorb a builder's balance of ready cash. In this context it must be appreciated that the days of the availability of credit from a large variety of sources were yet to dawn.

Reference to the list of vessels built by Barnard in this period, and his use of three separate building sites, would indicate that his capacity was stretched to the full and as such, in the prevailing conditions, he had become vulnerable. It is unfortunately difficult to prove that accumulated losses caused his collapse for it is not possible to match the Navy Bills he is known to have received with the vessels to which they applied.

Nevertheless an examination of Barnard's statements of account with the Alexander's Bank show an ever-deteriorating balance in the period from July 1778 to November 1781. A simple analysis discloses that net receipts from Navy Bills amounted to £27,795 whilst expenditure totalled £33,925, a deficit of £6,130. A sum approximating the £6,304 eventually paid out to creditors. An initial payment of ten shillings in the pound was made in 1785-6 and the balance in January 1789 (Appendix VII).

It is exceedingly difficult to translate the above-mentioned sums into late 20th century values with any degree of accuracy but if, for example, comparative wage rates are taken as a guide then the figure of £6,130 converts to an amount in excess of six million pounds. It must be emphasised that, at best, this is an approximation as so many different factors have to be taken into account but the sum does help set the bankruptcy in a calculated perspective.

Finally it becomes apparent that Barnard's failure was a matter of cash flow and liquidity rather than a question of his business liabilities outstripping the sum of his personal assets. He possessed and was copyholder of a considerable amount of property in Suffolk and Essex as well as owning the extensive freehold family residence with coach house, stables and greenhouses in the Parish of St Clement's. The list of his assets, publicly offered for sale by his assignees contained twenty separate lots, but not all had to be sold in order to cover his debts. In this context it is interesting to note that a number of properties were still in the hands of the Barnard family a generation later.

Even at this distance of time it is possible to feel the poignancy of his position. The disgrace and humiliation of finding himself both homeless and penniless after a lifetime of outstanding achievement must have been traumatic in the extreme. The words of his contemporary, Daniel Defoe, seem particularly pertinent:

"The best of men cannot suspend their fate" [60].

He died at the home of his son William in Deptford on 8 October 1784 in his 80th year.

It would be pleasing to think that in the few years left to him he found some satisfaction and consolation in the success which his son William had achieved in his own shipbuilding enterprises on the River Thames.

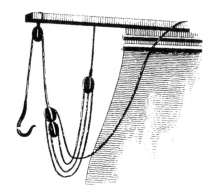

Chapter VII

William Barnard 1735-1795

William was the oldest surviving son of John Barnard the Younger; he was baptised on 9 June 1735 at the Dissenter's Chapel, Tacket St, Ipswich. Like his father and grandfather before him he was destined to become a shipwright and shipbuilder, as would his own sons in the course of time. It is probable, in view of the partnerships he joined later in life, that he served his apprenticeship in the Royal Dockyard, Deptford, but evidence of this has not been forthcoming. On 16 October 1760, at twenty five years of age, William married Frances Clarke, spinster, at the Church of St Saviour, Southwark; he was described in the register as a bachelor of the Parish of Harwich in the County of Essex. The entry is important in that it shows that he was then working with his father in the King's Yard, Harwich.

William would have commenced work at Harwich in or around the year 1756, and it is reasonable to assume that he continued working with his father until 1762, when, at twenty seven years of age, he decided to enter into business on his own account. The years 1756-63 coincided with those of the Seven Years War; so William would have gained valuable experience helping build the Naval vessels which flowed from the Harwich yard in those years. Nevertheless, working in his father's shadow could well have had its drawbacks for a young man of William's natural ability; so it was not surprising that when an opportunity to become his own master arose he took it with alacrity.

Partnership at the Nova Scotia Yard, Ipswich

In 1762 William entered into partnership with a William Dudman to build the *Speaker*, an East Indiaman of 700 tons, in his father's yard at Nova Scotia. It will be recalled that William's father became closely involved with the building of the said vessel. William Barnard took as his partner William Dudman. He was an experienced shipwright who, having served his apprenticeship in the Portsmouth Royal Dockyard, served in both the Plymouth and Woolwich Dockyards before being appointed an Overseer at the Deptford Yard. He was a native of Portsmouth and was forty three years of age when he joined William in Ipswich. He brought a great deal of experience but no capital into the partnership.

No evidence has survived in respect of the circumstances which brought the two Williams together but they could well have met if William Barnard had served his term of apprenticeship at Deptford as suggested.

Table VI
Merchantmen built by Barnard and Dudman at the Nova Scotia Yard, Ipswich

Name	Tonnage	Service	Commander	Launched
Speaker	700	East India Company	–	30.1.1763
Tuscany Frigate	–	Leghorn Trade	B. Cuite	12.8.1763
Dawes	300	Jamaica "	John Forbes	8.10.1763
*Africa**	–	Africa "	John Forbes	19.3.1764
Best in †				
Christendom	–	Jamaica "	Capt Barnard	1.7 1764
Dunkirk	300	Jamaica "	John Stevens	12.9.1764
Susanna †	300	Jamaica "	Capt J. Barnard	26.11.1764

Notes:
* *Africa* It was reported in the Ipswich Journal of 26 March 1764 that she was the first of her kind to be sheathed in copper.
† The Commanders of *Best in Christendom* and *Susanna*, Capt Barnard and Captain John Barnard (possibly the same man), have not been identified as being related to the Barnard family of Shipbuilders.

"A view from the waters of Messrs Barnard and Dudman's shipyard, Deptford" (John Cleveley). Exhibited by The Society of Artists, 1774

The *Speaker* was ready for launching on 30 January 1763, but as the following report in the Ipswich Journal of 4 February reveals, there were problems:

"On Monday last was launched here the *Speaker*, a fine ship of upwards of 700 tons, built by Messrs Dudman and Barnard Jnr. for the service of the Honourable East India Company. Being put off too hastily some time before high-water she stopped before she was clear of her ways; but the next day was got afloat with little trouble; and is now going down the river to Harwich in order to be rigged. The ship was begun 30 July last."

The *Speaker*, although by far the largest, was only one of seven vessels built by the partnership in the yard at that period. There is no evidence of John Barnard taking any interest in any of the vessels built other than the *Speaker*.

The Grove St Partnership

The year 1763 was a watershed in the lives of William Barnard and his partner William Dudman, for apart from being busily engaged in building the above-mentioned vessels, they took a step which, as far as William Barnard was concerned, severed all links with his father's businesses in Ipswich and Harwich. The break came when, late in the year 1763, the couple, together with Henry Adams of Beaulieu, took a 30 year lease from the Evelyn Estates of a shipyard in Grove St, Deptford, on the River Thames.

The Grove St Yard covered an area a little in excess of nine acres and was known on the Thames as the Lower Wet Dock, a title it was doubtless given to distinguish it from the far larger Howland or Greenland Wet Dock situated a little further up river. In order that it cannot possibly be confused with any other yard bearing the title 'lower', it will be referred to forthwith in these pages as the Grove St Yard. It consisted of two dry docks, one extensive wet dock and three building slips together with the usual installations. It was situated some three and a half miles down stream of London Bridge on the left bank of Limehouse Reach, being immediately south of the Surrey-Kent border and north of the Victualling Office and of the Royal Deptford Dock Yard. It had a river frontage of some 450ft and was situated at the very heart of merchant shipbuilding in the U.K. The density of the concentration of shipbuilders on this stretch of the Thames is exemplified by Daniel Defoe in his 'A Tour through the Whole Island of Great Britain', in which he observed that between Southwark and Blackwall there were three wet docks, twenty two dry docks and thirty builder's yards, all for the purpose of merchant shipping; the figure did not include builders of smaller craft.

Shipping on the Thames, Deptford

The partnership commenced trading in April 1764. In view of what was to occur in later years it is necessary to examine the manner in which the partnership was set up and the terms agreed. The offer of the lease was obtained by William Dudman at the latter end of the year 1763 from the attorney acting for the Evelyn Estates. Unfortunately the two Williams did not have sufficient capital to take up the offer. Dudman then approached Henry Adams of Buckler's Hard, Beaulieu, who agreed to join the partnership and to provide capital at 5%. It was also agreed that he would move from his home on the Beaulieu River to Deptford in order to play his full part in the management of the business. The verbal agreement between the three parties gave Adams a partnership share of one third of both profits and assets. Written articles of agreement were never drawn up, an omission which, in the course of time, would result in the partners becoming embroiled in the proceedings of the Court of Chancery. The partnership took over the lease of the Grove St Yard for the full term of thirty years, expiring on 25 December 1793.

Henry Adams was born in Deptford in 1713. His apprenticeship was served in the Royal Dockyard, Deptford, and completed in 1734. After working a further ten years in the same yard he was appointed Overseer at Buckler's Hard, a small shipbuilding yard

on the upper reaches of the Beaulieu River in the County of Southampton (Hampshire). In the course of time he commenced building for the Navy Board at Buckler's Hard on his own account. By the year 1760 Adams was a relatively rich man, but as few naval contracts were placed in the decade which followed, Adams thought it prudent to enter into partnership with Dudman and Barnard at the Grove St Yard.

As verbally agreed both Dudman and Barnard moved from Ipswich to Deptford; Adams, on the other hand, reneged on his promise to join them; it was a decision which contributed to the misunderstandings and mistrust which eventually destroyed the partnership. Although Dudman had no capital stake in the venture, as the older and more experienced man, he acted as senior partner or manager and, as such, lived with his family in the dwelling house on site. The first nine years of the partnership appear to have prospered as well and even better than might have been expected, the mainstay of the business at this juncture being a succession of building contracts for the construction of East Indiamen.

Attention must now be given to the fact that a great deal of confusion has arisen in published ship-lists relating to vessels built by the partnership in the Grove St Yard in the years 1765-1791, vessels seemingly being attributed to a number of different or individual firms.

The confusion arises because the firm was addressed in a variety of styles by different organisations or even differently by the same organisation. For instance the following forms of address are to be found in the Admiralty, Navy Board and H.E.I.C. records.

Adams and Barnard; Barnard and Adams; Henry Adams, Barnard and Dudman; Dudman and Co; Dudman, Adams and Co; Adams, Barnard and Co.

The point to be appreciated is that, whatever the form of address, all vessels either serviced or built in the Grove St Yard between the years 1763-1791 were solely for the partnership account.

Before moving on to the details of the ships built, a somewhat bizarre incident which occurred a little over a year after the formation of the partnership must be recounted. The story appeared in the Ipswich Journal of 8 June 1765 and is best told in the words of the reporter – a Gentleman of Veracity:

"A few Weeks ago a Person who call'd himself the Marquiss of Tolerado, and made a brilliant Appearance, applied to an eminent Broker in London, to recommend him to a Ship-builder, who would undertake to build some large Ships; The Broker recommended him to Messrs Barnard, Dudman, and Co. at the Greenland Wet Dock, Deptford, to whom he proposed the Building of six Ships of War of 1,000 Tons, and to carry 30 guns each, saying he was employed by the Corsicans: Mr Barnard objected to engage so many, but offered to contract for two, which Proposal was accepted, and he was ordered to make a draft of them as soon as possible, which was done in two or three Days, and the Marquis after examining them with great accuracy and the appearance of Knowledge in the Construction of a Ship made a small Alteration in the Breadth, and directed them to be put on the Stocks forthwith.

He then applied to Rope, Anchor, Mast-makers, &c, and gave Orders for such Things as were necessary to fit out the Ships.

In the mean Time the Broker hinted to him as he was a Stranger, it would be expected he should make a Deposit to the Contractors, which he said was very reasonable, and gave the Broker Bills on a House at Paris, to the amount of 6,000 l. for that Purpose, which for expedition and safety the Broker sent his Clerk to get accepted.

Soon after the Marquis sent for the Broker, and said he wanted a little ready Cash, and offer'd him an accepted Bill for 80 l. on the same House of Paris, which the Broker made no Scruple of giving him the Money for.

In a Day or two after the Marquis sent for him again, and wanted 80 l. more, which creating some Suspicions in the Broker, he said he had not so much Money on him, but would endeavour to get it for him by Night, and took occasion to ask him if he knew any Body in London, he said he knew some Persons in Publick Characters, and mentioned one to whom he said he was well known.

The Broker found Means the same Day to inform himself of his Character from the Gentleman, who said he believed he knew who he meant, and the less he trusted him the better: Upon this information the Broker took an Officer with him, and met him on his return from Ranelagh, with all the Parade of a pompous Equipage, Servants in Livery, &c.

The Broker charged him with being an Imposter, and demanded Satisfaction for the Money he had already advanced.

The Marquis talked in a high Strain for some Time; but finding him peremptory in carrying him to the Counter, he altered his Tone, and fearing, as is supposed, the return of the Clerk from Paris, he consented to have a Jewller and Taylor sent for, who appraised his Diamond Ring, gold headed Cane, and laced Cloaths, to nearly the Amount of the Money advanced, and thankfully receiving a Coat more suitable to his Circumstances, was permitted to go about his Business."

The interesting points to emerge from the story are that the Broker referred to the firm as Barnard and Dudman and that, after so short a time, the partnership was sufficiently respected in the City to be recommended to a seemingly valuable client in connection with what appeared to be an order of some magnitude.

The business conducted by the partnership at Grove St differed from that carried out by William's father at Harwich, in that, whilst the Harwich Yards depended almost entirely on Naval contracts, the business at Grove St became, in the course of time, divided evenly between Naval contracts and contracts for East Indiamen, the latter possibly proving the more lucrative in view of the amount of servicing and refitting which naturally resulted. In order to fully comprehend the close relationship which developed between the shipping interests of the H.E.I.C. and the merchant builders on the Thames it is necessary to have a basic knowledge of the manner in which the Company conducted its affairs. Due to the size and complexity of the subject only an outline of the Company's long and extraordinary history and its working practices can be given in these pages. Chapter VIII is devoted entirely to both aspects.

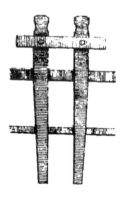

Chapter VIII

The Honourable East India Company

History [61]

The phenomenal growth and success achieved by the East India Company is unparalleled in the annals of private enterprise in this country. No other body of shareholders governed by a Court or Board of Directors ever reached the pinnacles of political power and military might which the Company in its heyday exercised on the continent of India. Queen Elizabeth I's Charter of 31 December 1600 conferred on 'The Governor and Company of Merchants trading into the East Indies' the sole right of trading with the East Indies for a term of fifteen years. The company was incorporated with a capital of £72.0.0 which was held by 125 Shareholders, the term East Indies being defined as all countries beyond the Cape of Good Hope and the Straits of Magellan.

In the course of its history the Company underwent metamorphosis after metamorphosis, changing its name, absorbing interlopers, increasing its capital, extending its activities and power until such time as it became a State within a State, a situation which, especially when its charter came up for renewal at twenty year intervals, attracted venomous criticism from those excluded from the lucrative India trade, and, as a result of such criticism, the control of Indian affairs eventually passed from the Company to the Government at Westminster.

The first expedition of four ships sailed from Torbay in April 1601 and returned with a cargo of spices from Sumatra in 1602. Further voyages were undertaken. The intrusion of these merchants into the eastern seas met with hostility from the Portuguese and Dutch who had earlier established trading stations in those waters. Nevertheless, in the years 1611 and 1612 respectively, the first British settlements were made at Madras on the east or Coromandel coast of southern India and at Surat on the north west or Malabar coast. In 1629 Surat became the seat of the Company's government in India. Madras was acquired by the Company in 1639 and was fortified as Fort George. To the north, at the mouth of the Ganges, a factory was established on the Hoogly River which was abandoned in 1685 following the Company's attempt by force of arms to coerce the Moghul Emperor to its wishes. In 1690 the factory was re-sited in a more favourable location and was fortified in 1694 to become Fort William. The city of Calcutta which grew around the fortifications became a presidency in 1700. Further territory was added to the Company's interests when, in 1668, Charles II presented it with Bombay, which he had received by way of a dowry from the Portuguese. At the end of the seventeenth century Bombay replaced Surat as the Company's seat of Government. The King also granted the Company further important charters which gave it the right to acquire territory, coin money, command fortresses and troops, form alliances, make war and peace and exercise both civil and criminal jurisdiction – powers which were synonymous with those of a sovereign state.

Towards the end of the eighteenth century, developments in Bengal led to Calcutta taking over from Bombay as the seat of the Company's headquarters in India. Warren Hastings was appointed the resident Governor General.

In the War of the Austrian Succession (1742-48), Britain and France were in opposing camps and, although it was a purely European conflict, France carried the war to India. She met with some success and Madras fell. It was, however, returned to Britain in 1748 by the terms of the Treaty of Aix-la-Chapelle. Robert Clive, the Company's most dedicated and celebrated servant, was, at the time, a junior clerk in the Madras office and was forced to flee and find refuge in Fort David. It was as a volunteer in the force which

East India House, 1815 (*Copyright © The British Museum*)

repulsed the French attack on the fort which first revealed his military potential and resulted in his receiving an ensign's commission. Conflict between Britain and France again broke out on the Indian continent over a local case of disputed succession. In this confrontation Robert Clive, in 1751, again distinguished himself by the capture and subsequent defence of Arcot, a town west of Madras. Victory over the French was achieved by Col Coote in 1761.

Previous to this victory the young Nawab of Bengal, Suraj-ud-Doulah, had quarrelled with the British and with a great army marched on Calcutta, an expedition which resulted in the death of a large number of innocent people in the so called 'black hole'. Robert Clive mustered a force which first recaptured Calcutta and then defeated Suraj-ud-Doulah at the Battle of Plassey, a victory which laid the foundations of the British Empire in India - the year was 1757. In 1760 Clive left India for Britain only to return five years later with the double appointments of governor and commander-in-chief. During his absence a decisive victory had been achieved at Buxar in 1764, when Major (later Sir) Henry Munro defeated a coalition of Indian forces invading Bihar. The victory determined British supremacy in Bengal. The new situation was confirmed in a treaty in which Shah Alam, having lost his gamble to support the ousted Viceroy's attempt to win back his power by force, gave the Company power to collect the revenues of Bengal, Bihar and Orissa.

The ceremony at which the relevant treaty was signed, as recollected by a Mohammedan contemporary, appears to have been a somewhat bizarre affair; it took place in Clive's tent on a throne which consisted of a chair set on an English dining table covered by an embroidered cloth. The document, signed by Robert Clive and Shah Alam, made the Company de facto rulers of 30 million subjects yielding an income of four million pounds sterling. The aforementioned Mohammedan contemporary's comments on the occasion are both amusing and illuminating; he wrote "the transaction was done and finished in less time than would have been taken up in the sale of a jack-ass".

Sad though it is to relate, this glut of easy money had a most deleterious effect on the Company's servants and brought about the most shameful period in the Company's long association with India. Many employed in the Company's service were not slow to take advantage of the rich pickings available, and with their pockets lined with ill-gotten gains returned to England as rich men. Lord Clive summed up the situation in a few well-chosen words:

"I will only say that such a scene of anarchy, confusion, bribery, corruption and extortionwas never seen or heard of in any country but Bengal, nor such and so many fortunes acquired in so unjust or rapacious a manner."

The old East India House, 1648-1725 Leadenhall St London (*Copyright © The British Museum*)

Famine in India added to the misery of the peasants and rising military expenditure in Bengal reduced the Company to the verge of bankruptcy. A request to the Government at Westminster for a loan resulted in a wide-ranging enquiry which brought in its train the Regulating Act of 1773; this gave the British Government partial control over the Company's servants and revenues. Eleven years later Pitt's India Act of 1784 ensured Parliamentary supervision over Bengal through a Board of Control under the presidency of a Government appointee. India was, thereby, ruled by the British Government through Company Agency. In 1813 the Company's monopoly of trade with India was ended and in 1833 the Company's monopoly of trade with China, mostly in tea, was also terminated. The final charter expired in 1874.

Freight, ships and shipping

The main homeward-bound cargoes were, in the seventeenth century, Indian cotton, and in the eighteenth tea from China. Other freight would have consisted of indigo, saltpetre, pepper and Chinese raw silk and porcelain. All had to be purchased with bullion as there was no demand for European goods in the

The Directors Court Room, New India House
(*Copyright © The British Museum*)

Auctions were a regular feature of India House
(*Copyright © The British Museum*)

exporting countries. Cargoes, on arrival in this country, were sold by auction in the Company's London warehouses. The growth in the numbers employed overseas by the Company brought about an ever-increasing passenger traffic on both outward and home-bound ships, a factor which led to the development of vessels which were a combination of merchantmen and passenger-ships, an unusual hybrid at that date. In addition, because of the danger of attack by pirates and enemy privateers, East Indiamen were far more heavily armed than the usual run-of-the-mill merchantmen.

The ships were a credit both to the Company and to the shipbuilders who designed and built them. Sir Evan Cotton, in the Introduction to his "East Indiamen", wrote:

"No finer fleet of merchantmen ever sailed the seas than that which carried the trade of the Honourable East India Company."

In size, East Indiamen increased with the passing of the years, say from an average of some three hundred tons in the second half of the seventeenth century up to over one thousand tons in the late eighteenth century, while individual ships, destined for the China trade, had a tonnage of say fourteen hundred tons. In appearance East Indiamen were not dissimilar from ships of His Majesty's service, and although they were no match for more heavily armed men-o'-war their look-alike aspect, on more than one occasion, confused and deceived a more powerful adversary.

Apart from a relatively short period in its early days, the Company did not build or own ships in which it carried out its business; it entered into charter arrangements with private owners. Such owners being a syndicate or body of shareholders headed by an individual known either as the managing owner or the ship's husband.

Ships' husbands

The ship's husband was the pivot around which the so-called shipping interests of the H.E.I.C. revolved, for not only was he responsible for arranging the building of the ships (with the contract being made out in his name), but he was also the authority who arranged its charter with the Company, agreed the number of voyages to be made and dealt with all matters concerning the freight to be carried. The remaining shareholders, usually prominent men in the City of London or from other spheres of life, were non-executive, being content to receive any dividends which might or might not be payable on their investment. With the passing of time the role of the ship's husband became something of a profession in its own right, with individual husbands becoming managing owners of any number of ships; for instance in the eighteenth century Charles Raymond was husband to a total of twenty four ships. Not surprisingly, as the vested interests of both husbands and shipbuilders were similar, a close relationship sprang up between the two parties.

It is probable that William Barnard and his successors held shares in the East Indiamen they built. Specific bequests of such shares are to be found in the wills of William's widow Frances and of his partner William Dudman.

The permanence of a 'ship's bottom'

In simple terms the expression 'to build on a ship's bottom' had, by the eighteenth century, come to mean replacing a vessel which had either been lost at sea or had become worn out. Company custom and practice brought about a situation whereby a replacement vessel automatically inherited the rights of the vessel she was replacing, which meant that once a vessel was accepted for charter she was assured of an active career before even having her keel laid, subject, of course, to there being sufficient trade for her employment. 'Bottoms', like shares, were marketable. This situation gave husbands an almost complete monopoly over the ships being chartered to the Company, a monopoly which was largely concentrated on the River Thames.

It will be seen that sitting at the centre of this monopolistic merry-go-round were the River shipbuilders. They were in a fortunate and even formidable position; for neither the Company nor the husbands could easily fulfil their proper functions without a convenient supply of suitable vessels. A requirement the River shipbuilders were only too ready to meet. So close did the personal and financial links between the builders and the husbands become that, for a time, the husbands refused to consider tenders from builders outside the River and the shipbuilders, for their part, refused to build East Indiamen for anyone other than their accepted customers. In modern times this might be referred to as a closed shop within a closed shop.

The Barnards and their husbands

An analysis of the East Indiamen built by the Barnards between the years 1763-1825 shows that at least sixty nine vessels were built on behalf of thirty seven different husbands. Of this number approximately one third contracted for more than one ship. Robert Williams, and his son of the same name, were pre-eminent in this respect; for they contracted for ten or

possibly eleven ships between the years 1777 and 1808. It must further be appreciated that the launch of a vessel did not necessarily mean that a builder had seen the last of that particular ship for it was customary for a ship to return to its home yard for cleaning, repairs or refitting after each passage to and from the East. For example, the last ship built by the Barnards for the Williams family - the *Princess Amelia II* - enjoyed a service life of some seventeen years, making in all ten voyages, her last commencing in 1825. The association between the Barnard and Williams families would therefore have extended for some fifty years, for the first vessel built by the Barnards for the Williams made her maiden voyage in 1777.

Chapter IX
The Grove St Partnership

The thirty year partnership at the Grove St Yard, Deptford, between William Barnard, William Dudman and Henry Adams fell into three distinct stages. The first stage, 1763-72, was somewhat blighted by Henry Adams breaking the verbal partnership agreement to join his fellow partners at Grove St in order to assist in the conduct of the business, instead he remained at his own yard at Buckler's Hard, on the Beaulieu River. He nevertheless retained a financial interest in the Grove St Yard. Despite his absence the two Williams prospered. In the summer of 1772 William Dudman died.

The second stage 1772-79, thereby, fell squarely on the shoulders of William Barnard who not only continued to contract with the shipping interests of the H.E.I.C., as in stage one, but also commenced contracting with the Navy Board.

In 1779, William Barnard, on his own account, purchased a lease of a shipyard at Deptford Green owned by the Bridge House Estates. He retained his partnership at Grove St and for the next ten years he controlled both yards. John Dudman, son of the late William Dudman, managed the day to day affairs of the Grove St Yard.

The remaining three years of the partnership witness a clash of interests which led to an acrimonious legal battle.

Grove St 1763 -72

In retrospect it might be thought hazardous to have commenced trading in the year 1764, for the Peace of Paris, which ended the Seven Years War, had been signed in 1763, thereby bringing to an end the flow of Navy contracts to the merchant builders in the war years. Only one order for a ship of the line was placed in 1763, and that was received by the Royal Dockyard at Chatham. No orders were placed in the year 1764 and only five for the year 1765, none of which were received by merchant builders. It was not until the year 1771 that the Navy Board again called on the merchant builders for assistance. Notwithstanding the absence of naval orders, the partnership commenced trading with contracts received from the shipping interests of the H.E.I.C.

There can be little doubt that one reason for the success of the partnership in securing contracts was the excellence of the facilities of the Grove St Yard; for in addition to the dry dock and building slips, common to most merchant yards on the Thames, it also had the benefit of its wet dock, a facility which gave the yard maximum flexibility in the handling of vessels brought in for repairs and refits. It would have been one of the three wet docks in the hands of merchant builders on the Thames reported by Daniel Defoe in his 'A Tour through the whole Island of Great Britain', referred to earlier in these pages.

Seven East Indiamen, all attributed in the H.E.I.C. records to Dudman [62] were launched in this period. In addition the yard would have received contracts from other sources, and would certainly have been engaged in the tasks of cleaning, repairing and refitting vessels, including, as the following letter shows, ships of His Majesty's service. A letter from the partnership to the Navy Board signed by William Dudman, dated 23 April 1771, is of special significance in that it highlights the interplay of interests between the yard and its customers.

The letter reads:

"Honourable Sirs,
I humbly request the favour of the Honourable Board, to be permitted to undock His Majesty's Ship *Levant* on Tuesday next, the 30 instant, and put her into the Wet Dock to finish her, having but little work to do on her, and that whole inside work. I should not have troubled the Honourable Board, but if we omit docking an East Indiaman the next Spring we shall lose the fitting of her, and likewise the owner's future favours. If agreeable to the Honourable Board, please to send an order to the officers of His Majesty's Yard, to assist with people, and a large chain lighter to lift her abaft; having no ballast, will draw a very considerable difference of water. Should have waited on Your Honours to request this favour, but have been so ill could not possibly get up so far, and Mr Barnard being ill abed.
I am, Honourable Sirs, your most obedient humble Servant,

William Dudman."

An endorsement on the letter shows that having considered the matter the Board instructed its Secretariat to:

"Acquaint them we have no objection thereto, and that we have given orders to Deptford officers to assist with people and the large chain boat as directed. Give orders to Deptford officers accordingly" [63]

The *Levant* was a 6th rate of 28 guns, and it is not without interest that she had been built by Henry Adams in his yard on the Beaulieu River in 1758.

The incident emphasises, in the clearest possible manner, the prime importance the partnership placed on its H.E.I.C. connections. It is also pleasing to see the Navy Board so willing to co-operate, although, in so doing, it meant additional work for the officers of the Deptford Yard.

The seven East Indiamen launched in this period were:

Table VII
East Indiamen launched in the Grove St Yard 1765-1772

Date	Name	Bm	Husband
*1765	*Ponsbourne*	676	Thomas Lane
1767	*Granby*	786	Charles Raymond
1769	*Bridgewater*	804	John Wood
"	*Resolution*	826	Mark Cramer
1771	*Royal Henry*	842	Thomas Lane
"	*Royal Charlotte*	855	Albert Nesbit
1772	*Ankerwick*	763	Barrington Buggin

* Note: Thomas Lane would contract for a second *Ponsbourne* in 1780.

It will be appreciated that it was general practice for East Indiamen to return to the yard in which they were built for cleaning, repairs and refitting. On average, an East Indiaman made at least four return voyages, each lasting say two to three years, so that everything else being equal, the partnership was ensured of a great deal of future business from each East Indiaman it built.

His Majesty's Ship *Hector*

As stated above, the Navy Board did not contract with merchant builders for ships of the line in this period until 14 January 1771 when contracts for three 74-gun ships were placed with merchant yards. The partnership was indeed fortunate to be one of the favoured, receiving a contract for the *Hector*, which was laid down in April of that year. It may be recalled that John Barnard, at Harwich, also won a contract for the *Sultan* on the same date thereby giving the Barnard family the honour of building two-thirds of the vessels ordered.

An intriguing insight into the supply and demand of shipwrights on the Thames, when both the Royal Yards and merchant builders were competing for suitably qualified men, is to be found in two letters dated 26 and 28 October 1771 [64]. The letters happily disclose a pleasing degree of co-operation between the two parties. It would appear that the Royal Yards had loaned a number of their shipwrights to the Grove St

partnership in order to complete the building of the East Indiamen *Royal Henry* and *Royal Charlotte II*. The letter of 26 October was a plea that eight of the men due to return to the Royal Yards - out of a total of twenty - be allowed to remain for another month on the grounds that 'the work we have in hand for the East India Company's service requires a still great number'. The letter stated that failure to meet the contract date for completion would bring heavy penalties. The Navy Board generously compromised on the matter, allowing five of the eight to remain.

The incident, once again, emphasises the importance the partnership placed on the East India Company connections.

An unhappy turn of fate brought the first phase of the partnership's tenure of the Grove St Yard to an abrupt end when, in the summer of 1772, William Dudman died at the relatively early age of fifty two years. His practical knowledge and his wide experience of shipbuilding on the Thames played an important role in the success enjoyed by the partnership in this opening period.

His death must have come as a great personal blow to William Barnard; for evidence points to the two being close friends in spite of the difference in their ages. William Barnard was the sole surviving executor of Dudman's will, (proved 12 Sept. 1772), in which, in a codicil, he bequeathed "Unto the said William Barnard the sum of five guineas to buy himself a ring." He left a son, John, and five daughters.

As the elder and more experienced man, William Dudman had acted as senior partner. His death made William Barnard, then thirty seven years of age, entirely responsible for the conduct of the business. Subsequent events show that both in character and technical ability he was capable of dealing with all aspects of management.

Chapter X
The Grove St Partnership

Grove St 1772-79

The second stage of the partnership's tenure of the Grove St Yard, although relatively short, proved to be a period of intense activity, for a total of twelve vessels were launched in a seven year period compared with only seven vessels in the previous eight years. The increase was the result of the receipt of eight contracts from the Navy Board.

On the death of William Dudman, Henry Adams hastened from his yard on the Beaulieu River to Deptford. He did not stay for any length of time but returned home having, quite properly, demanded a statement of the partnership accounts at the date of William Dudman's death. The accounts, prepared by the firm's counting house, showed that the business was indebted to each of the three partners to the sum of three thousand four hundred and eighty one pounds twelve shillings and nine pence. In the case of Adams this was increased to eight thousand three hundred and seventy four pounds fifteen shillings after taking into account

the sums owed him on account of the timber and other materials he had supplied; it is probable that it also included any capital he had loaned to the firm [65].

At some unspecified date, William took into partnership John Dudman, the son of his late partner, who had been working at Grove St during his father's lifetime. The new partner was given a one fifth share in the partnership and allowed to continue living in the family home - the Builder's House on site.

Letters to the Navy Board

Once again very little is known of the problems which arose during the building of the eight naval vessels as, only four letters to the Navy Board have survived [66].

The first letter, dated 23 February 1776, was a somewhat testy epistle from William complaining that he had not been invited to attend a meeting, along with other River shipbuilders, at which tenders were to be made for a new bomb-ship. His irritation clearly shows in the closing words of his letter:

Table VIII
Naval vessels built at Grove St 1771-1779

Name	Rate	Guns	BM	Ordered	Launched
Ambuscade	5th	32	684	1771	17.9.1773 fir built
Hector	3rd	74	1622	14.1.1771	27.5.1774
Experiment	4th	50	923	1772	23.8.1774
Hound	Sloop	14	305	30.10.1775	8.3.1776
Pelican	6th	24	520	24.7.1776	24.4.1777
Hydra *	6th	24	454	1778	8.8.1778
Zephyr*	Sloop	14	187	1779	31.5.1779
Pandora †	6th	24	520	11.2.1778	17.5.1779

Notes:
*Both the *Hydra* and the sloop *Zephyr* were purchased by the Navy Board whilst on their stocks. The *Hydra* had been laid down as an East Indiaman.
The 24-gun frigate *Pandora* achieved lasting fame by playing out the last act of the drama of the Mutiny on the *Bounty*. Dispatched by the Admiralty in October 1790 in an attempt to round up the mutineers believed to be living on Tahiti and adjacent islands, she was wrecked on the Barrier Reef whilst attempting to pass through the Torres Straits at the northern tip of Queensland. Four of the fourteen captured mutineers were drowned together with thirty one members of the crew. The survivors, ten prisoners and eighty nine crewmen, made passage to Timor - some 2100Km. distant, in the ship's open boats. In November 1977 divers located the wreck site. A limited amount of excavation has taken place and a number of important artefacts recovered. Further excavation is planned when funds permit. She is declared 'an historic shipwreck', under the Australian Shipwreck Act (1976). Her discovery has aroused similar interest in Australia to that given to the *Mary Rose* in the U.K. (Appendix IX).

"...we have never shown any backwardness to attend your Honours on such business but have with unwearied application extended ourselves to the utmost in executing our late contract, we cannot account for the slight hereby put upon us, having hitherto, with pleasure reflected on transactions with the most impartial public body in the kingdom."

The reply, if any was made, has been lost.

The second letter, dated 3 August 1778, deals firstly with the intended date of launch of the *Pandora* in December 1778. It further makes a tender for a ship of 32 guns to be built on the slip vacated on her launch. It would appear that this tender was successful; for in Table X it will be seen that the *Orpheus* 32-gun was launched 3 June 1780.

The third and fourth letters, dated 6 August 1778 and 7 July 1779 respectively, deal with the ever-present problem of the wrongful impressment of shipwrights working on naval vessels in merchant yards. The letter of 6 August reveals a major breach of the regulations by the impressment officer:

"Honourable Sirs,
Joseph Dyer, shipwright employed by us on his Majesty's ship *Hydra*, being impressed and on board the *Nightingale*, the Proper Officer refusing to release him, having wrested his protection from him and destroyed it, we pray your Honours will order his discharge, the other shipwrights refusing to return to their work which they left yesterday. We are, Honourable Sirs,
your most obedient,
Humble Servants

Adams, Barnard & Co." (67).

The letter of 7 July 1779 was a request for the discharge of shipwright James Cook, also wrongly impressed and taken aboard the *Conquistador*. In both cases it must be assumed that the Navy Board complied with Barnard's requests.

East Indiamen

The four East Indiamen built in this period were for a new set of husbands. Both George Ramsay and Sir Richard Hotham would order one further vessel whilst the Williams family would order a further nine.

Table IX
East Indiamen built at Grove St 1777-1778

Date	Name	Bm	Husband
1777	*Mount Stuart*	758	George Ramsay
"	*Royal Admiral*	914	Sir Richard Hotham
"	*Royal Bishop*	720	Robert Williams
1778	*General Barker*	758	J. Durand

* Notes: i. The *Royal Admiral* was sold by Sir Richard Hotham to the Larkins family. After 18 year's service as an East Indiaman she was bought by the Navy Board for conversion to a 3rd rate of 64 guns whilst on the stocks in a Barnard Yard for servicing.

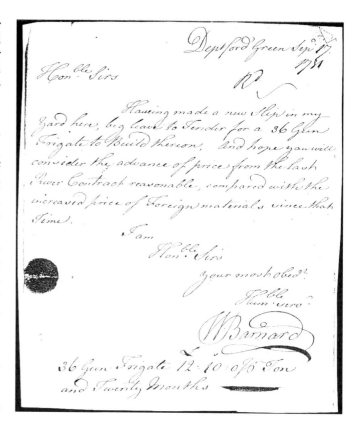

Letter of complaint from William Barnard in respect of failure to be asked to tender for a bomb ship

The wreck and salvage of the East Indiaman *York*

"On the 1st January 1779 in a most dreadful storm the *York* East Indiaman, homeward bound with a cargo of pepper, parted her cable in Margate Roads and was driven on shore within one hundred feet of Margate Pier."

The above quotation is taken from a paper written by William Barnard and read to the Royal Society by the then Astronomer Royal, Nevil Maskelyne, on 22 December 1779. The paper bore the heading:

"An account of a Method for the safe Removal of ships that have been driven on shore and damaged in their bottoms, to places (however distant) for repairing them" (Appendix X).

Sir Richard Hotham, friend and client of William Barnard, was the ship's husband. The *York* was on her fourth return voyage from the Far East. The prospect of losing both the ship and her valuable cargo at a point so near home must have been an agonising experience for Sir Richard and his body of shareholders. In desperation he appealed to William Barnard for help.

A summary of the events set out in the paper shows that on arriving at the site of the wreck, some three days after she had stranded, Barnard found that, whilst the *York* lay upright, she was stuck fast in a bed of chalk and clay to a depth of some 12ft and that her rudder had been torn away leaving her stern and bottom so badly holed that she flooded some 18ft at every tide.

Ambuscade is lost to French corvette *Bayonnaise*, 14 December 1798

His first action was to lighten her by removing all accessible cargo and to pump out any water remaining in the vessel at low tide. To help prise her from her glutinous bed of chalk and clay he stuffed inflated sheep-skins, sewn into sails, beneath her sides at low water and waited upon the rising tide to lift her. The ploy succeeded. Once the cargo was removed he calculated he would be able to move her into deeper water, subject, of course, to her being sufficiently watertight, which she most certainly was not. Holes in her sides and stern could be plugged with little difficulty, but her badly-damaged bottom was irreparable. His solution was both novel and ingenious; he constructed what amounted to a watertight 'box' low down in her hull so that, even with a holed bottom, she would float. The carefully-calculated dimensions of the watertight box provided sufficient displacement and stability for her to float. The experiment proved highly successful and the *York* was

towed to safety in Barnard's dry dock on the Thames.

Barnard's own words in the paper explaining the box-like contraption were:

"...The whole formed a compleat (sic) ship and flat bottom within to swim the outside leaking one; and that bottom being depressed six feet below the external water resisted the ships weight above of equal to five hundred and eighteen tons and safely conveyed her to Deptford...."

The reaction of Sir Richard Hotham to the success of this unusual salvage exercise is not known; but the favourable outcome brought its own small reward, for Barnard was asked to salvage a Swedish ship stranded near Margate during the same storm. The events subsequent to her stranding contained an element of farce, for she became wedged 'partly within and partly without' Margate Pier, where she had been abandoned by 'some of Ramsgate men' who had been vainly attempting to move her from her original point of

a)

b)

Drawings by Thomas Rowlandson 1782
a) Going on board the *Hector*, Man of War
b) Middle deck of the *Hector*, Man of War

stranding into the safety of Margate Harbour. Applying much the same principles, Barnard moved her safely into his yard in Deptford.

The year 1779 was also the year in which William Barnard took the first step which, in the short term, made him independent from the partnership although remaining a member of it, but which, in the long term, would lead to friction and disbandment.

In November 1779 he purchased on his own account for the sum of four thousand pounds at a rent of one hundred and fifty pounds per annum, the remainder of the lease of a dockyard in Deptford Green, the property of the Bridge House Estates. In 1786 the lease was renewed for a period of sixty three years (Appendix XI). The purchase did not preclude him remaining the managing partner at Grove St. In this context it must be recalled that, throughout the life of the Grove St partnership, Henry Adams continued to run his own yard at Buckler's Hard.

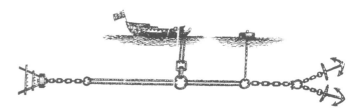

Chapter XI

Deptford Green and Grove St Yards, 1780-1790

The penultimate stage of William Barnard's shipbuilding career proved to be the busiest of his life, for the demand for Naval vessels and East Indiamen continued unabated, a total of forty one vessels being launched from the two yards in the eleven year period. William, as manager of both, was forced to assume the character of a juggler for although the yards were separate businesses, there was a maximum amount of collaboration between the two.

The Deptford Green Yard was situated approximately a quarter of a mile downstream of Grove St at the northern extremity of Deptford Creek, where an electricity power station now stands. The site, as a shipyard, was of some antiquity and is clearly delineated in a pen and ink drawing of Deptford dated 1623 which was later annotated by John Evelyn the diarist. If the account of the origin of the site given by Nathaniel Dews in his 'History of Deptford' (1884) may be taken at its face value it would appear to be the site purchased by the original East India Company in the reign of Queen Elizabeth I for the construction of its early vessels [68].

In 1779 the facilities on the site consisted of a dry dock and two slips together with all the necessary installations, including a substantial dwelling house and garden for the builder; a lesser house and garden was provided for the foreman and his family. The yard had a river frontage of some 344ft and a maximum depth of 731ft. In 1781 Barnard added a further slipway giving him, in all, three building slips and a dry dock.

During his tenancy the yard was known either as Mr Barnard's Lower Dock or often simply as the Lower Dock or Yard. Henceforth, it will be referred to in these pages as the Deptford Green Yard.

Table X
Naval vessels built 1780-1790

Name	Rate	Guns	BM	Ordered	Launched	YARD
Tortoise	Lighter		109	1780	17.7.1780	D.Gn
Orpheus	5th	32	688	2.10.78	3.6.1780	G.St
Africa	3rd	64	1415	11.2.78	11.4.1781	"
Andromache	5th	32	683	1.2.80	17.11.1781	"
Scipio	3rd	64	1387	11.11.79	22.10.1782	D.Gn
Carnatic	3rd	74	1703	14.7.79	21.1.1783	G.St
Iris	5th	32	688	5.10.81	2.5.1783	G.St
Inconstant	"	36	890	1782	28.10.1783	D.Gn
Tremendous	3rd	74	1651	30.6.79	30.10.1784	"
Solebay	5th	32	683	1.12.80	26.3.1785	G.St
Majestic	3rd	74	1623	23.7.81	11.2.1785	"
Zealous	3rd	74	1607	19.6.82	25.6.1785	D.Gn
Orion	3rd	74	1646	2.10.82	1.6.1787	G.St

NOTE: The *Orion* fought in more major battles than any other Barnard-built ship: she saw action at the Glorious First of June 1794, the Battle of Cape St.Vincent 1797, the Battle of the Nile 1798, Trafalgar 1805 and Copenhagen 1807. She was broken up in July 1814.

G St = Grove Street
D Gn = Deptford Green

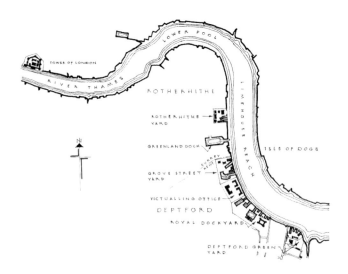

Location map of the Barnard shipyards on the Thames

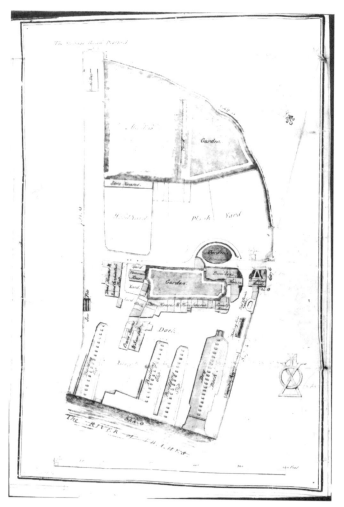

The Deptford Green Yard
(*The Corporation of London Records Office 280 No: 59*)

An analysis of the 42 ships launched from both yards in this period shows that thirteen were naval vessels and 29 East Indiamen. Unfortunately, in respect of East Indiamen, it is impossible to identify the yard of their origin, as the surviving H.E.I.C. records only refer to them as being built on the Thames. In the case of naval vessels sufficient evidence exists to make the required identification. In order to simplify tabulation, separate ship lists have been drawn up for naval and East Indiamen.

The Navy Board and the launch of the *Tremendous* and *Majestic*

It will be recalled the American War of Independence was virtually brought to an end by the surrender of General Cornwallis at Yorktown on 17 October 1781. The four 3rd rates *Majestic*, *Tremendous*, *Zealous* and *Orion* had been ordered between the years 1779-82 and were not due for delivery until dates which proved to be after the signing of the Peace of Versailles by which Britain recognised the independence of the United States. An unforeseen and most unfortunate result of this situation was that the Navy Board found itself in a position whereby, for financial reasons, it had to inform Barnard that the delivery dates of the *Tremendous* and the *Majestic*, as stated in the contract, would have to be put off for a number of months. The letter which set the whole episode in motion was a routine communication written by Barnard on 9 August 1784 informing the Board that the *Tremendous* would be ready for launching from the Deptford Green Yard on 30 October 1784 and the *Majestic* on the 27 November 1784 from Grove St. The Board replied on the same day informing him that the launching of both ships would have to be delayed until some unspecified date in 1785. This most unwelcome information, coming so late in the day, must have struck Barnard with the force of a thunderbolt, for the prospect of having two 74-gun ships occupying his main building slips until well into the New Year had frightening implications.

The problems facing Barnard were practical, but with financial consequences in that he had already entered into contracts to build vessels on the slips he had expected to be vacated. In the field of finance the delay meant that the final instalments due on both vessels would not be forthcoming until the day of their launch. Barnard would, therefore, have to find the wages of the workforce of both vessels, together with the cost of material purchased in the final stages of construction. Furthermore, this interruption in his anticipated cash flow presented problems in respect of the payment for the timber and material he had contracted to purchase on account of vessels he had contracted to build. There was also a question of insurance, for the £20,000 cover he had taken out on

1799, HMS *Tremendous* with HMS *Adament* 50 guns chases and drives ashore the French frigate *Preneuse* in Tombeau Bay, Mauritius

both the *Tremendous* and *Majestic* was due to expire in the months of November and December.

All these points were made clear in a letter to the Board dated 10 August 1784. He also drew the Board's attention to the fact that although he had kept them fully informed of the building progress in respect of the two vessels in question there had never been any suggestion that the launching dates would be delayed. An appeal to the Board's honour, in which he reminded them that "...as he had done all in his power to fulfil his side of the contract then the Board should be ready to comply with theirs" fell on deaf ears. A personal meeting with the Board brought him no comfort and left him sadly remarking that "little remains to be said of the business."

However, notwithstanding the rebuffs received, he made yet another attempt to coax the Board to a more reasonable state of mind. His letter of 12 August, written only three days after the affair first came to a head, concluded with the words:

"Your Honours will, after mature deliberation determine the short question whether the Service shall suffer a temporary inconvenience which it was not with me to prevent, or the ruin of an individual in his fortune and reputation (after having performed all that could be expected on his part) which must inevitably take place if the *Tremendous* is not permitted to launch the 30th October and the *Majestic* the 27th December next, had I more slips I should be happy to meet the views of the Board as far as circumstances would admit, but I hope that from their known Justice, and Candour, they will not expect from me more that it is possible in my situation to perform."

It would appear that the Board made no reply to this letter, for Barnard wrote yet again on 20 August requesting permission to launch on the original dates. The Board replied on the same day suggesting that the launch should go ahead as planned, thus freeing the slips for new building, but with the proviso that no final payments would be made by the Board until the

naval estimates for the year were made known. This posed two problems: firstly, the date of publication of the naval estimates might be months ahead and secondly, the peace-time naval estimates might be so reduced as to make it difficult for the Board to meet its commitments. Barnard made a counter proposition that he would launch as agreed, but that payment should be guaranteed before the end of January 1785 [69].

The Board's reply is not known, but the *Tremendous* was launched on the due date of 30 October 1784; however, the launch of the *Majestic* was delayed for reasons unknown until 11 February 1785. It must not be overlooked that during this time the *Zealous* and the *Orion* were still on their stocks. They were launched in June 1785 and June 1787 respectively. They were the last naval vessels built by William Barnard, as he did not participate in the building programmes initiated by the Navy Board at the onset of war with Revolutionary France in 1793.

Miscellaneous Navy Board 'In Letters' 1781-1783

Some seventeen of William's letters to the Board have survived for this period [70]. The first, written from Deptford Green Yard and dated 17 September 1781 informs the Board that:

"Having made a new slip in my yard here, beg leave to tender for a 36 gun frigate to build there-on and hope you will consider the advance price from the last River Contract reasonable compared with the increased price of foreign materials since this time."

The price quoted was £12.10.0 per ton with a twenty month date of delivery.

The letter is of particular interest for it is linked with other letters in the same batch, firstly in its reference to the increased price of materials and secondly in the outcome of the offer to build a frigate.

With regard to the increase in the price of materials it may be recalled that William's father, John Barnard,

HMS *Inconstant*, a needlework picture in wool

3 February 1814, HMS *Majestic* in action with two French frigates and an American privateer
Artist: G Gilbert Eng. C Hunt

had been made bankrupt as a result of inflationary pressures, and that William Barnard was appointed as assignee. As such he, with his coassignees, was made responsible for the completion of the *Irresistible* building at Harwich. The Navy Board, it would appear, became dissatisfied with the speed at which the assignees were proceeding. In reply, William's letter of 25 March 1782, set out the problems and assured the Board that:

"I have used every means in my power for her dispatch and that the limited nature of my situation as an assignee would permit, and have supplied a great many of the more difficult articles from my yard here, to my great disadvantage and hindrance and without any possible pecunary assistance from the creditors."

His closing words have a touch of pathos in view of the relationship between the assignees and the contractor.

"... trusting you will not be severe on the creditors of an old and unfortunate contractor if they should exceed the time allowed."

The episode in respect of the tender for a frigate had its amusing side, for William completely over-reacted to the Board's refusal to consider his terms. He erroneously believed that he was being severely censured as a result of his failure to meet delivery dates on a number of his contracts. In order to vindicate his position as a good responsible contractor he wrote to the Board on 1 October 1781 setting out the dates of delivery, before and after contract, of the nine vessels built by the partnership in the Grove St Yard. The analysis disclosed a thirteen month difference in favour of early delivery although only three of the vessels were, in fact, delivered prior to their contract date, as the following extract from the letter shows:

Table XI
Ships built for his Majesty's service by Adams Barnard & Co. in the River Thames.

Name	Date of contracts	Time allowed	Time of Launching	Before or after contract	
Hector	Feb. 18 1771	42 months	May 27 1774	2 months 20 days	Before
Ambuscade	Feb. 20 1771	24 months	Sep. 17 1773	7 months	After
Experiment	Dec. 12 1772	30 months	Aug. 23 1774	9 months 17 days	Before
Hound	Nov. 6 1775	March 31	March 8 1776	23 days	Before
Pelican	Aug. 6 1776	Dec. 1777	Apr. 24 1777	8 months 7 days	Before
Pandora	Feb. 16 1778	15 months	May 17 1779	1 day	After
Africa	Feb.16 1778	36 do.	Apr. 11 1781	23 days	After
Orpheus	Oct. 9 1778	18 months	June 3 1780	1 month 26 days	After
Andromache	Feb. 16 1780	15 months	will launch Nov. 3rd.	15 months 13 days	After
Scipio	Dec. 9 1779	36 months	Shall be launched in time		
				Months	(Days)
			Whole time before contract	22	( )
			Whole time after contract	9	( )

The irony of the situation is exposed in an endorsement to the letter written by a seemingly somewhat perplexed member of the Navy Board, which read:

"Inform him that our only objection to giving him a frigate is the number of ships he has in hand, but as he has no frigate at the yard where the *Scipio* is building, we will agree with him for a 30 gun ship, at the usual price by the draught of the *Andromache*."

There is no record of William Barnard's response.

Other letters in the batch deal mostly with matters of routine such as offering to tender for a 74-gun ship to be built on the slip to be vacated by the *Scipio*; offering the Navy Board a vessel already building on the stocks to the lines of an East Indiaman and due to be launched in 'September next', and making preliminary arrangements for the repair of frigates in both the Deptford Green and Grove St Yards.

East Indiamen 1780 - 1790

A total of 28 East Indiamen and one hoy for the Company's service were built in the yards in this period. The ship-list shows that they were built for twenty two different husbands, most of them contracting for one vessel apiece, exceptions being James Farquharson and William Larkins who contracted for two apiece, and Robert Williams who contracted for seven.

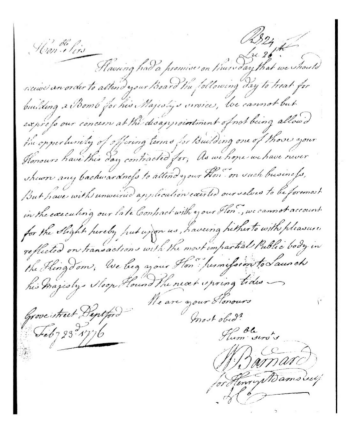

Tender for a 36 gun frigate to be built on a new building slip at Deptford Green

Table XII
East Indiamen built 1780-1790

Date	Name	BM	Husband
1780	*Hinchbrook*	528	Robert Williams
"	*Modiste*	1004	?
"	*Neptune*	809	Andrew Moddat
"	*Ponsbourne*	750	Thomas Lane
"	*Sulivan*	876	Robert Williams
1781	*Antelope*	270	Capt Henry Williams
"	*Brilliant*	730	Sir William James
"	*Dutton*	761	Capt Henry Rice
"	*Fairford*	790	George Ramsay
"	*General Coate*	787	Robert Williams
"	*Warren Hastings I*	763	William Larkins
1782	*Winterton*	876	Thomas Newte
1783	*Middlesex*	825	Robert Williams
1785	*Bridgewater*	799	Nicholas Skottowe
"	*Rockingham*	798	Sir Richard Hotham
1786	*Clinton*	711	William Larkins
"	*Earl Fitzwilliam*	803	James Farquharson
"	*Marquis of Lansdown*	574	Anthony Brough
"	*Mars*	696	Capt Wm. Farrington
"	*Madras*	hoy	East India Service
"	*Melville Castle*	806	David Webster
"	*Princess Amelia*	808	Robert Williams
1787	*Airley Castle*	803	Robert Williams
1787	*Boddam*	1021	William Palmer
1787	*Enfield*	1021	?
"	*Prince Wm.Henry*	803	James Farquharson
1789	*Hindustan I*	1248	Robert Williams
1790	*Arniston*	1200	John Wedderbourn
"	*Taunton Castle*	1209	Peter Esdale

Boats from HMS *Orion* rescue crew of *Margarite and Ann* as her foremast catches fire 16 leagues south of Iceland, 1808 (Jorgen Jorgensen)

The East Indiaman *Dutton* 1781 - 1796

As will be seen from the ship-list the *Dutton* was built in 1781 for the account of Capt Henry Rice. She is of particular interest to this history in that Thomas Barnard, the son of John Barnard the Younger by his second wife Sarah, and therefore a step-brother of William Barnard, signed on as fifth mate on 31 December 1784. It was the first step in a successful career in the Company's service for, in the course of time, he attained the rank of Captain. He was the only member of the shipbuilding branch of the Barnard family known to have made seafaring his career. On his retirement he joined the mast-making side of the family's shipbuilding business and will appear later in this work.

The *Dutton* also has her own particular niche in the maritime history of this country as a result of the heroic efforts of Capt Edward Pellew (later Admiral of the Fleet Viscount Exmouth), then on shore leave, to rescue successfully hundreds of soldiers trapped aboard her as she lay wrecked and pounded by the storm below the Citadel in Plymouth Sound on 26 January 1796. The *Dutton* was acting as a chartered troop-carrier, and was part of a large fleet returning from the West Indies.

"Success to Mr Barnard's Yard"

These words of goodwill are inscribed on the inner base of a Chinese Export Porcelain Presentation Bowl of the Qianlong Period (c1785) now in the possession of the National Maritime Museum, Greenwich. The bowl first made its appearance from a source which, to date, has refused to be identified, in the showrooms of Messrs Lawrence of Crewkerne in 1987. It was subsequently sold to Messrs Spink and Son in 1988, who in turn sold it to the National Maritime Museum. It is in an excellent condition with no restoration and only a small fragment of un-glaze on its foot. It is unique in that it is the only bowl of its type known to have been dedicated to a merchant builder. The outer face of the bowl depicts a number of vessels in frame form, as if awaiting launch, set against an oriental river background. At first sight the vessels might be thought to be but figments of the Chinese artist's imagination; but research has shown that they are, in fact, exact copies of drawings to be found in Chapman's 'Architectura Navalis Mercatora' published in Stockholm in 1768 (Appendix XII).

There can be little doubt that the bowl was either ordered by or made for presentation to the William Barnard of this history, for the period of the bowl, and the years of William's close involvement with the shipping interests of the H.E.I.C., exactly coincide. It may well be that the bowl was made to celebrate the acquisition by William of the Deptford Green Yard.

The pristine condition of the bowl shows it to have been carefully tended throughout the two hundred years of its existence, a fact which could point to its having been in the possession of a so far unidentified branch of the Barnard family.

H.M.Customs

In 1785 William Barnard had the honour of being appointed sole shipwright to H.M. Customs for the Port of London. Unfortunately the Customs Records for the period were destroyed by enemy action in World War II. It is not known what exactly the appointment entailed. The natural assumption would be that vessels for the service were built, cleaned and repaired by the appointed sole shipwright of the day. Quite apart from the importance of the appointment in terms of shipbuilding his choice as sole shipwright indicates the high esteem in which William Barnard was held on the River.

The *Hindustan I* made her first trip to China in 1790, leaving the Downs 17.01.1790 and returning to Deptford 17.07.1792. The artist, Thos Luny, was on the voyage

The wreck of the *Dutton* at the foot of the Citadel, Plymouth Sound, 26 January 1796

The Partnership - the final years

The lease of the Grove St Yard was due to expire on 25 December 1793. It would appear that prior to this date there was considerable discussion between the partners as to whether the partnership should be put into liquidation and the resulting funds distributed or whether it should continue in being. It will be readily appreciated that the three had opposing interests; Adams, who was very comfortably placed in his yard on the Beaulieu River, no doubt considered his investment in Grove St not only as an additional source of income but also as an outlet for timber and other merchandise in which he traded. He, therefore, would have no wish to see the partnership dissolved. John Dudman, as junior partner, with no financial stake in the enterprise, other than his small share of the profits, was dependent on the business both for his livelihood and for his place of residence. John Dudman would, therefore, also have favoured renewal. On the other hand, William Barnard, not unnaturally, wished to divest himself of the heavy burden of managing the Grove St Yard from which, it must be remembered, he received only one third of the profits.

The unhappy path down which this conflict of interests led make up the final years of William Barnard's shipbuilding career and, it is sad to relate, of his life.

Henry Adams (1713-1805)

Chapter XII

The Grove St Partnership

Dissension, dissolution and death 1790-1795

The last five years of William Barnard's relatively short life must have been difficult years indeed; for not only was he battling with his partners in the Courts to protect his rights but, from 1793 onwards, he was a sick man. The nature of his illness is not known. He died on 6 March 1795 in his 60th Year.

This sad state of affairs would appear to have adversely affected his shipbuilding for, after a spate of building in the previous decade, no naval vessels were launched in the years 1787-1793 and no East Indiamen in the years 1790-5.

William Barnard's last letter to the Navy Board was dated 20 May 1790 and concerned the provision of protections for his shipwrights engaged in repairing frigates in his Deptford Green Yard [71].

The first indication that his health had deteriorated to any great extent is contained in a letter dated 2 June 1794, written by his eldest son William, then a nineteen year old apprentice in his father's yard.

The letter reads:

"Hon Sirs,
I beg leave (for my father) to inform you that he intends launching the stationary floating battery on Saturday the 14 inst. provided that day meets Your Honours approbation, as she will then be in all respects complete.

I am......
William Barnard" [72].

Dissension

As has been previously stated, the issue of the future of the partnership arose some two years prior to the expiry of the lease in 1793, and although there are no records of the initial discussions which took place, it is obvious that there was a great deal of ill feeling between the three men. An impasse would seem to have been reached early in 1792 which resulted in William Barnard taking unilateral action by writing to both Adams and Dudman giving notice of his resignation from the partnership, a course of action he was fully entitled to take. His letter of resignation to Henry Adams read:

"Mr Henry Adams, I do hereby give notice that the partnership now subsisting between you, John Dudman and me, the undersigned William Barnard, in the trade and business of shipbuilding under the style and firm of Adam, Barnard and Dudman, shall cease and be determined on the first day of March next ensueing the date here of

Signed William Barnard
10 Feb. 1792" [73].

The reply made by Adams was as unexpected as it was unjustified; for he made the extraordinary claim that the Deptford Green Yard was part and parcel of the partnership assets and, as such, would have to be included in any liquidation. Whether or not Adams really believed what he claimed or whether it was just a ploy to force Barnard to change his mind will never

Table XIII
Naval vessels built 1790-1795

Name	Rate	Guns	Ordered	Launched
Spanker	Floating battery	24	1794	*14.6.1794
Diamond	5th	38	2.3.93	17.3.1794
Dryad	5th	36	24.5.94	4.6.1795
Kite	Brig Sloop Fir, Built	16	1795	17.7.1795
Sylph	Brig Sloop Fir, Built	18	13.7.95	8.9.1795

be known; but in this context it must be borne in mind that for the eleven years that Barnard had leased the Deptford Green Yard Adams had never questioned the fact that Barnard was the sole lessee. Whatever his intentions, the claim made by Adams had one devastating effect. Barnard's hands were tied until such time that Adams either withdrew his claim or Barnard could prove his case in a court of law. Adams did not withdraw, which left Barnard with the only option open to him, which was to take the case to the Court of Chancery.

The proceedings of the Court of Chancery, immortalised by Charles Dickens, were notoriously cumbersome and were conducted within a rigid and time-consuming framework. Cases were heard by the Court through the medium of Bills or Affidavits which were exhibited by both the plaintiff and defendant. A case was initiated by the plaintiff exhibiting a Bill of Complaint. In reply the defendant would exhibit his own case in a Bill known as an Answer. Further Bills from each side would follow in a seemingly-unending stream, with the result that a case could remain before the Court for years on end. In this instance, five Bills were exhibited, one of which was amended and re-exhibited, making a total of six Bills in all. They were [74]:

7 March 1792	William Barnard's Complaint against Adams and Dudman, amended 13 May 1793.
19 May 1792	Henry Adams Answer
23 June	William Dudman's Answer
27 June	Henry Adams Complaint against Barnard and Dudman
16 October	Barnard's Answer

In addition to the foregoing Bills, the 'Entry Books of Degrees and Orders of the Court' contain a number of petitions by the litigants requesting permission for further action, which in each case were granted, thereby extending any deadline previously imposed by the Court in respect of individual Bills.

Space does not permit even a cursory examination of the many claims and counter-claims made in the aforementioned Bills; but as the dispute involved the very future of the Barnard family's standing on the River it is vital to understand the issues at stake.

Stripping away all questions of a peripheral nature, and there were many, the issue which dominated the whole affair was the ownership of the Deptford Green Yard.

In his Bill dealing with the question, Barnard pointed out that it was only after he had made clear his intention to dissolve the partnership that Adams made any suggestion that the partnership had an interest in either the lease or in the business of the Deptford Green Yard. Barnard also reminded Adams that both yards

The *Spanker*, Floating Battery

* Note: The *Spanker* was an innovative vessel. She was intended as a formidable naval weapon and built to carry mortars and guns of a large calibre, her dual task being to assist the fleet in the bombardment of land-based fortresses and to act in a defensive role in harbour protection. She was some 111ft 6ins in length with the unusual feature of having a rectangular main deck projecting over her lower works, on which her full complement of twenty four guns were mounted. Unfortunately such an ungainly vessel proved unseaworthy and she was retained solely for harbour service, becoming a hospital ship at Sheerness only a year after her launch.

had their own counting-houses and employed different clerks, and that separate books of account were kept by the said clerks; furthermore that all contracts, receipts and other business papers were made out either in the style of Adams, Barnard and Dudman or simply William Barnard according to the yard to which the particular business applied. In this context it is interesting to note that Naval records show that the Admiralty clearly considered that it was dealing with two separate and distinct businesses.

Adams, amongst the legion of charges he levelled against Barnard (which included theft, lying and conspiracy to defraud) accused him of using partnership monies to purchase the Deptford Green Yard, a charge Barnard rigorously and convincingly refuted and offered to have books of account produced for the Court in order to confirm his memory.

Dissolution

The case was eventually settled out of court in February 1794, but the terms of the settlement are not known. However, subsequent events show that the partnership must have, in fact, been dissolved on the due date of 25 December 1793; for from that date John Dudman took over the lease of the Grove St Yard in his own name and held it until 1813. The lease of the Deptford Green Yard remained in William Barnard's name until his death in 1795 and, furthermore, it remained in the name of the Barnard family until its expiry in 1849. Henry Adams, who appears to have gained nothing whatsoever from his possibly vindictive behaviour, continued to live at Buckler's Hard until his death in 1805.

HMS *Dryad*, 36 guns, bringing to close action the French frigate *La Prosperine*, 40 guns, off Cape Clear, West Indies during the war against revolutionary France 1793-1802. Captain: Lord Amelius Beauclark. *La Prosperine* suffered 30 killed and 45 wounded (Thos. Whitcombe)

Death of William Barnard 1795

William Barnard died from his illness in the very first days of March 1795 and was buried in the burial ground of the Meeting House, Butt Lane, Deptford. His address given in the Burial Register was the Builder's Yard, Deptford Green. He left a wife, Frances, two sons, William and Edward George, together with three unmarried daughters, Ann, Frances and Elizabeth.

In his will he bequeathed:

"...all my Freehold Farm called Cookes Green in the Parish of Little Clacton in the County of Essex....my two Copyhold Farms in the Parish of Great Holland...and also my Freehold Messuage in Butt Lane, Deptford and all Real and personal Estate whatsoever and wheresoever unto my beloved wife Frances Barnard for her absolute use and benefit and disposal and constitute and appoint her sole Executrix."

The will was signed and sealed on 23 February 1795 only a week before his death. It was proved in London on 7 March 1795.

The lease of the Deptford Green Yard, at William's death, had a further fifty four years to run. The records

of the Bridge House Estates show that in 1796 the name of their tenant was changed to that of the widow, Frances Barnard; it remained in her name until her death in 1825 (Appendix XIII).

The Navy Board was informed of William's death by his eldest son William Barnard Jnr, who at the time would have been nineteen years of age; it was certainly the most poignant letter, dated 4 March 1795, written by a member of the Barnard family to the Board in the 100 years or more of their business relationship. It read:

"Honourable Sirs,
While I inform Your Honours of an unfortunate event, the death of a Father, permit me to solicit a continuance of your favours on behalf of my Mother who will carry on the Business for the benefit of herself and family (with assistance of a very able foreman who served his time to my father and who has acted as foreman under him upward of twenty years, and who since his long and unfortunate illness of more that twelve months has conducted the whole of the business). Until myself and brother shall have served the remainder of our apprenticeship and shall be in a situation to join her.

1851, Portsmouth Harbour. HMS *Victory* saluting Her Majesty Queen Victoria. From 1838 the hulk *Dryad* was used for harbour service. The steam-yacht in left background is HMS Yacht *Fairy*

That no opportunity will be omitted on her part to render herself worthy of your honour's patronage I can take it upon myself to assure your honours, and that it will be her constant study to show her gratitude by a diligent, punctual and conscientious performance of any contract with which your Honours may favour her...

I have the honour to be with great respect
Honourable Sirs,
Your most obliged, humble servant,
William Barnard"[75].

The young man's plea did not go unheeded; for the Navy Board continued to contract with the family until the end of the Napoleonic Wars, when contracting-out to Merchant Builders came to an abrupt end. Furthermore his father's connections with the shipping interests of the H.E.I.C. remained intact.

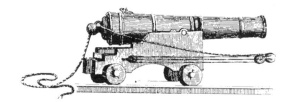

Chapter XIII

Frances Barnard Sons & Co. 1795-1805

Frances Barnard was fifty eight years of age at her husband's death and as sole beneficiary of her husband's estate she inherited the lease of the Deptford Green Yard and, in so doing, became de facto senior partner of the firm. It is doubtful whether she played an active part in the day-to-day affairs of the business, as in 1803 she moved to Ravensbury Manor House, Mitcham, in the County of Surrey, where she lived in considerable style. There are, however, indications that she exercised a measure of control through her hold on the purse-strings.

Her two sons, William and Edward George, were both serving their apprenticeships at the date of her husband's death and were respectively aged approximately nineteen and seventeen years of age. It is not known when their apprenticeships expired; but assuming that both would have qualified by their twenty first birthdays, then they could have taken up partnerships in the business in December 1797 and May 1799 respectively, a supposition to some extent confirmed by the fact that up until January 1798, letters to the Navy Board were signed Frances Barnard and Co. but by March 1801 the firm styled itself Frances Barnard Sons and Roberts. It is not known when Mr Roberts joined the partnership or from whence he came.

The death of William coincided with a critical period in the history of this country; for turbulent events were being enacted on the continents and oceans of the world. In 1793 England had joined a coalition in a war against Revolutionary France which raged until 1802 and which gave rise to such maritime actions as Admiral Lord Howe's victory on the Glorious First of June 1794, the first fleet action against Revolutionary France; the defeat of the Spanish fleet off Cape St Vincent in 1797; the destruction of the French fleet at the Battle of the Nile in 1798 and the Battle of Copenhagen

Table XIV
Naval vessels built 1795-1805

Name	Rate	Guns	Ordered	Launched
York*	3rd	64	–	24.3.1796
Triton	5th	32	1795	5.9.1796
Crash	Gun vessel	12	7.2.1797	5.4.1797
Contest	"	"	7.2.1797	11.4.1797
Adder	"	"	7.2.1797	22.4.1797
Spiteful	"	"	7.2.1797	24.4.1797
Northumberland	3rd	74	10.6.1795	2.2.1798
Eolus	5th	32	1800	28.2.1801
Locust**	Gun-brig	12	30.12.1800	2.4.1801
Mallard	"	"	30.12.1800	11.4.1801
Repulse	3rd	74	4.2.1800	21.7.1803
Harrier	Brig-sloop	18	1804	22.8.1804
Elk	Brig-sloop	18	1804	22.8.1804

Notes:
* The *York* was the converted East Indiaman *Royal Admiral* building on the stocks in 1795.
** It should be noted that the *Locust* is incorrectly attributed to Randalls of Rotherhithe by J.J. Colledge in his 'Ships of the Royal Navy'.

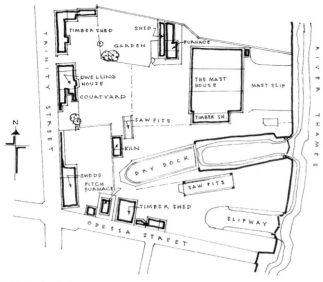

THE BARNARD ROTHERHITHE YARD

in 1801. The Treaty of Amiens signed in 1802 brought an end to hostilities. The peace did not hold. Napoleon's overwhelming military supremacy in Europe and his refusal to negotiate certain withdrawals demanded by the English brought about a renewal of hostilities in 1803. In the following two years, Napoleon threatened to invade England, a threat which caused the Government and the people of this country considerable disquiet. The 'Army of England', an invasion force of some one hundred thousand men backed up by seven hundred shallow-draught barges, was stationed at Boulogne. Unfortunately the naval force necessary to protect the invasion fleet during the Channel crossing was not forthcoming. Notwithstanding Nelson's decisive victory over the French and Spanish fleets at the Battle of Trafalgar in 1805 the Admiralty could not relax its vigilance; for whilst Napoleon remained supreme in Northern Italy and the Netherlands his shipbuilding capability was as great, if not greater, than that of England. The demand for additional naval vessels by the Admiralty remained unabated. A situation wholly favourable to the merchant builders. Napoleon was finally defeated at the Battle of Waterloo in 1815. He was exiled to the island of St Helena, and with his very considerable suite was trans-shipped to the island aboard the 3rd rate *Northumberland*, a vessel launched by Frances Barnard, Sons and Roberts in 1798.

William Barnard 1795-1805

Very little is known of William Barnard beyond his shipbuilding activities. The records show that on 11 February 1799 he married Harriet Goodwyn, daughter of Henry Goodwyn, a brewer, (resident of Blackheath) at the church of St Botolph-without, Aldgate, in the

City of London. The couple had three children, Frances, William Henry and Thomas. Following their marriage the couple lived at The Yews, Croome Hill, Greenwich. He may also have been the William Barnard who, in 1798, enlisted in the Corps of Volunteers raised in Deptford to protect the local populace from the threatened French invasion. In business William appears to have inherited the natural skills of his shipbuilding predecessors; for although he unfortunately died in February 1805 at only twenty nine years of age he achieved a large measure of success during his years of stewardship.

Notwithstanding his overall success the contribution made by the firm to the war effort was not outstanding; a fact which was again due to the commitment to East Indiamen. Thirteen contracts were completed for the Navy Board - mostly small vessels such as gun vessels and sloops but the list did include two 3rd rates of 74 guns. On the other hand a total of fifteen vessels were built for the shipping interests of the H.E.I.C., of which four were East Indiamen of over one thousand two hundred tons. The building of twenty five vessels in eleven years with the relatively limited facilities available must have called for a high standard of management.

Navy Board 'In Letters'

The conversion of the East Indiaman *Royal Admiral* to the 64 gun *York* produced a most singular state of affairs in respect of the cost and payment of the conversion, especially in view of the inviolability of Naval Contracts. A letter to the Navy Board, dated 17 September 1795, disclosed an astonishing error on the part of Frances Barnard & Co.

The letter read:

"We hope your Honours will excuse us troubling you relative to the payment of the 64 gun ship *York*, late *Royal Admiral*, East Indiaman, for the contract being copied from an original one for a ship built some time since the payments were also copied without considering the increase price per ton for the present ship and that at finishing the ship there will be a balance of £5,240. We therefore hope your Honours will indulge us by adding £1,500 to the next payments which will make the sum received by us an amount equal to which Messrs Randall, Brent, Sons will receive for their ship.

Signed Frances Barnard & Co." [76].

No record exists of the Navy Board's immediate reply to this somewhat naïve plea; however, fourteen months later on 11 November 1796 (some six months after the actual launch of the *York*) the firm again wrote to the Board as under:

"We have received your Honour's Letter of 4th August Instant and we are extremely sorry that whatever stated in our letter of the same day will not induce you to alter the mode you have determined upon the settlement of our

Bonaparte being transferred from the *Bellerophon* to which he had surrendered, to the *Northumberland* which took him to St Helena, 8 August 1815

account for the sixty four gun ship. We lament that we are again obliged to object to such terms but as it is our wish to avoid dispute with your Honours we beg leave to say that we are very ready to submit our will to the arbitration of any proper judge that may be appointed between us and we hope that this proposal may meet your Honours on the subject.

Frances Barnard & Co" [77].

Whether or not the matter went to arbitration is not known; but in December 1796 the Board wrote to the firm complaining that the said conversion appeared to be proceeding at too slow a pace. In a letter dated 30 December 1795 Messrs Frances Barnard & Co replied that:

"The great difference in materials necessary for a ship of war from those previously provided for the ship as an East Indiaman and the great delay all our business met with when, in common with other builders, thought it necessary to resist the exorbinate (sic) demands of our sawyers, together with a variety of alterations that have to be made to frames and other parts of her construction are principle reasons that the York is not in a forwarder state...." [78].

The letter then went on to assure the Board that every conceivable step was being made to have the

vessel ready for launch in March 1796. She was, in fact, launched on 24 March 1796.

The reference to resisting 'the exorbinate demands of the sawyers' is also of interest as it foreshadows the far more serious trouble which developed on the River some six years later.

Triton lying-to 1796 (Pocock)

East Indiamen

It is unfortunate that no information has come to light in respect of the actual building of East Indiamen in the Barnard yards; but the pattern and daily routine of their building would have been similar to that of naval vessels, as would have been the problems which would have arisen. The reason for this lack of information is that all questions relating to the construction of a vessel would have been addressed to a ship's husband, which means that unless such information is to be found in the private papers of a said husband there is little prospect of enlightenment. On the other hand contracts between husbands and builders have, in a number of cases, survived, so that the exact dimensions and all other details of the vessels construction are open to inspection.

In the case of the Barnard-built East Indiamen at least one contract has survived. It is for the *Preston* and is between Frances Barnard and Co and William Hamilton Esq, merchant of Mincing Lane, London [79]. It is dated 24 February 1795 (Table XIV).

The *Hindustan II* and the *Walmer Castle* (Table XV), built respectively for Robert Williams and J P Clarke, were two of the largest East Indiamen built in the Barnard yards; the former made four successive voyages to China before being lost on 11 January 1803 in a heavy gale on the Wedge Sand, losing between twenty five and thirty of her crew.

Extracts from the log of her last voyage give an exact account of her progress on both the outward and homeward journeys:

Leave Portsmouth 18 March 1797 - at Bombay 4 July
at Cochin 18 Oct - at Malacca 8 Jan 1798
at Whampoa 3 March
- off Nankas 26 April - at Angar 17 May - at St Helena 5 Aug
- at 'the Downs' 18 Oct - at Long Reach 22 Oct
Arrive Deptford 23 Nov. 1798

The round voyage took approximately twenty months, and on her return to Deptford she would have been taken in by the Deptford Green Yard for cleaning and repair. Her next voyage to China departed from Portsmouth on 18 June 1799.

The Mast Yard Rotherhithe

In late 1798 or early 1799 William Barnard and his younger brother Edward George purchased from the Wells family (an old established shipbuilding family on the River) certain freeholds in Rotherhithe which were located some four hundred yards upstream of the Greenland or Howland Wet Dock and about three and a quarter miles below London Bridge. The yard had a river frontage of some four hundred and fifty feet and a depth of approximately the same. Contemporary maps show, that it was bounded to the West by Upper

Table XV
East Indiamen built 1795-1805

Date	Name	Tons	Husband	Voyages
1795	Walmer Castle	1460	John P. Larkins	9
1796	Hindustan II	1463	Robert Williams	6
1797	Caledonian	612	Robert Charnock	2
1798	Preston	679	William Hamilton	6
1798	Varunna	526	John Princep	?
1799	Earl St Vincent	818	John P. Larkins	7
1799	Lord Nelson	819	Robert Charnock	5
1800	Dorsetshire	1201	Robert Williams	9
1801	Baring	819	Robert Charnock	6
1802	Warren Hastings II*	1276	John P. Larkins	2
1802	Bentley	Hoy		
1804	Metcalf	819	James Thomas	6
1804	Phoenix	818	Robert Williams	6
1805	Sir William Pultney	565	John Locke	6
1805	William Pitt	819	Henry Bonham	7

NOTE: Tonnage as per Register, Master attendants Office [80].
* The *Warren Hastings II* was engaged in a most memorable sea battle against a more heavily armed French adversary, *La Piémontaise* (Appendix XIV).

The 44-gun American frigate *Constitution* out manoeuvres the more lightly armed British frigates during the war with America of 1812

East Indiaman *Warren Hastings II*

Trinity St and to the south by Odessa St. A field, with an area of some five hundred and fifty feet by three hundred and fifty feet, located on the opposite side of Upper Trinity St, was included in the purchase. The shipyard consisted of a large dry dock and building slip but, most important of all, it possessed mast making facilities in a mast-house and mast slip. The art of mast-making fell within the province of the shipwright. It was a highly specialised procedure calling for particular skills. The new yard considerably widened the scope of the business; for masts would be made for all and sundry and not restricted to Barnard built ships. Furthermore the additional dry dock and building slip substantially increased the firm's building capability and made it possible to carry out a greater number of repairs and refits. The building programmes entered into for the years 1800 - 1805 could not have been completed without the facilities of the newly purchased yard.

The mast making business was carried out as a separate entity, the partners being Frances, Thomas, William and Edward George Barnard. According to contemporary Business Directories, Edward George Barnard, the owner of the yard, leased it to the aforementioned partnership. Thomas, it may be recalled, was the step-brother of William (I) and had spent most of his life in the service of the H.E.I.C.

Inflationary pressure and social unrest

Inflation at differing rates and in many guises is a by-product of most wars. The wars against France were no exception. It will be recalled that John Barnard the Younger had been bankrupted by being trapped between fixed price contracts and rising prices at the time of the American War of Independence. By the year 1801, the inflationary pressures on the merchant builders on the River became so onerous that, in concert, they took the unprecedented step of writing to the Navy Board soliciting relief. A contemporary copy of their letter has survived, which unfortunately does not give the names of the signatories, dated 11 January 1801, it read:

"Honourable Sirs,
We Presume to solicit your attention to the following statements that we the Undersigned have endeavoured to prove ourselves valuable servants to the public by executing important contracts with punctuality and honour and a view to very inadequate profit. That our later engagements to build 74-gun ships we are confident will be a ruinous concern, the 74's built by us previous to the last barely saved us from loss and by reductions of the size of the present may be considered as being of the same price and materials and labour having risen on an average of 16% there is a certainty of a loss to attach, which we hope the Hon Board will consider and grant us such relief as their liberality may judge proper. We are informed a shipbuilder in the country has

been advanced 10/- on our price tho' it was a practice of the Hon Board previous to this was to allow 7/6 per ton at least difference in favour of the River builders, the saving in freight of timber alone being very considerable. We hope we shall stand excused for intruding on the time of the Board by the present application which we have composed in as few words as we could and want to give any explanation of the grounds of it that may be required" [81].

Their plea did not fall entirely on deaf ears as the following letter, dated 20 January 1801, shows. Addressed to Messrs Perry, Wells Green, it reads:

"In return to you and the other shipbuilders letter of 11 instant representing that you should sustain a very great loss by completing your present engagement for building the 74-gun ships for His Majesty's service and praying that some relief may be granted you. We acquaint you that when the ships are launched any circumstances you may have to state on this subject will be taken into serious consideration.

We
Your affectionate friends
C.Hope
J.Henslow
W.Bellingham" [82].

The final outcome of their plea is not known; but as there were no bankruptcies on the River at that time some compromise must have been reached. However, be that as it may, the matter was still very much alive in 1803; for in that year there is a memo from the Deptford Green Yard to the Navy Board concerning the contents of the said letter and its probable whereabouts [83].

The twin problems of the lack of profitability resulting from naval contracts in times of high inflation and the need of the workforce to demand compensation for the rise in the cost of living by demanding higher wages were certainly not new to the shipbuilding industry.

The previously-mentioned "exorbinate demands of the sawyers" made in 1795 had, by 1802, developed in open confrontation between the employers, the sawyers and their fellow shipwrights, the caulkers. By the end of July the situation was out of control and violence threatened. The trouble, as far as Frances Barnard and Co were concerned, centred around twenty five caulkers, innocent parties who had been temporarily transferred from the Royal Yard to take the place of strikers who had been working on the naval vessels then in the Deptford Green Yard. On 28 July 1802 Messrs Frances Barnard and Co wrote to the Navy Board reporting a disturbing and deteriorating situation:

"After applying at the Public Offices we this morning got thirty men from the Thames Police and twelve from Union St to protect men Your Honours was so kind to order from the King's Yard, 25 of which was intended to come to us from the Deptford Yard. We applied this morning for the men informing them we had protection enough to take them to our yard, a great number of caulkers and sawyers being assembled, as on Monday and Tuesday, near the yard. They informed us that they were fearful of their lives and refused to come, Mr Tippets, the Master Shipwright, was present and informed us he would write you on the business" (84).

This letter, supported by others from fellow merchant builders on the River, together with a number from the officers of the Deptford and Woolwich Royal Yards, were sufficient to goad the Navy Board into action. It promised that "by Tuesday next a sufficient force will be provided to protect the caulkers in going to merchant yards and during the time they continue there" (85). Furthermore, the Navy Board stated that any Royal Dockyard caulkers refusing to comply with the order would be immediately discharged. As pawns in the dispute the Royal Dockyard caulkers seem to have been between the devil and the deep blue sea. The protection offered was confirmed by the Secretary of State, who informed the merchant builders that both civil and military assistance would be made available (86).

The correspondence does not reveal exactly how much of the promised protection actually materialised or how, when and where it was directed. It certainly did not immediately resolve the dispute because about a month after the above-mentioned letter from Messrs Frances Barnard & Co was dispatched, John Dudman, writing from the Grove St Yard, reported highly riotous behaviour by the striking caulkers. His letter, dated 21 August 1802 gives a graphic description of the events of the day:

"I beg leave to inform you that this morning at about half past ten o'clock a body of River caulkers, in number about 100, overpowering the Porter, who was placed at the Gates of the Yard, entered the yard and went on board His Majesty's ship *Septre* and forcibly obliged the caulkers belonging to His Majesty's Yard at Chatham, who were at their work, to come ashore....I immediately went to their assistance and found the whole body descending the Brow, I expostulated with the Chatham caulkers, promising them all the protection in my power and endeavoured to persuade them to return to work but finding they declined so to do on being intimidated by the threats of the others I then ordered the Gates of the Yard to be secured in order to gain time to procure assistance from His Majesty's ship *Diligance*, before such assistance could arrive, they, in opposition to all resistance myself and officers could make, forced the Gates of the yard by breaking the Bar to which they were chained, they then forced seven of the Chatham caulkers out of the yard and took them off in a most insolent and riotous manner towards Deptford" (87).

The outcome of this show of force is not known; but by the end of October 1802 the differences between the warring parties had been resolved. On the 29 of that month Messrs Frances Barnard Sons & Roberts were writing to the Navy Board thanking them for their assistance and at the same time praising the Dockyard caulkers 'who obeyed the orders given with pleasure, kept constant to their work, (which they executed in a workmanlike manner) although often abused, insulted and threatened by the riotous people which had left our employ' (88).

William Barnard (II) died in February 1805: the cause of his death is not known; but he was only twenty nine years of age. It may well be that he became afflicted by some recognisable terminal illness; for his last will and testament was dated 5 January 1805, only a few weeks before his death. He was buried, on 17 February 1805 in the burial ground of the Meeting House, Butt Lane. His address in the burial register was given as 4 Builder's Yard, Deptford Green.

His will, proved at London 25 February 1805, was very specific in respect of the manner in which his half-share of the Rotherhithe Yard should be dealt with on his death (89). He firstly bequeathed his share to his cousin Edward Clarke with the proviso that should his co-shareholder, Edward George, wish to purchase the said half-share within a period of twelve calendar months then he might do so provided that the sum paid to Edward Clarke was the same as that paid to Messrs Wells. Edward George exercised the option and thus became the sole owner of the Rotherhithe Yard.

Chapter XIII

Edward George Barnard

The fatal years 1805-25

Following the death of William, his younger brother, Edward George, took over the management of the business and the style of the firm became Frances Barnard, Son and Roberts. Edward George was then twenty seven years of age and unmarried. Frances Barnard remained at her home at Ravensbury House, Mitcham, in the County of Surrey.

In the ten year interval between Nelson's victory at Trafalgar in 1805 and the defeat of Napoleon in 1815 the Admiralty, for reasons already stated, embarked on an extensive building programme which included the building of fifty nine 3rd rates of 74 guns, of which thirty six were built in merchant yards. The firm of Frances Barnard, Son and Roberts received its fair share of the business; laying down six naval vessels between the years 1805-10, of which four were 3rd rates of 74 guns. They were the last naval contracts received by the Barnard family.

It is also of interest that of the five 3rd rates, ordered by the Navy Board on 31 January 1805, four of the contracts were granted to families of the original Grove St partnership, contracts being awarded as under

Marlborough	Frances Barnard Son and Roberts
Sultan and *Royal Oak*	Dudman and Co
Hannibal	Henry Adams, Buckler's Hard.

Navy Board 'In Letters'

The number of letters relating to the above building programme are few in number, and deal mostly with matters of routine [90]. Two, however, are worthy of note.

The first, written on 28 August 1807, was a somewhat plaintive plea to be given a contract for another 74-gun ship; which, it would appear, would be in addition to one already ordered and possibly on the stocks. The grounds for such a plea were that other merchant builders on the River had been so favoured. The letter unfortunately also contained the stipulation that, due to other commitments, completion could not be expected for some three and a half years. The Board's curt endorsement on the said letter read:

"Acquaint them that the time they ask for building a 74-gun ship being more than any other builder we cannot take their offer into consideration."

A letter of 22 February 1809 appears to show that somewhere along the line there was a change of mind, for it discloses that the Board had directed that the *Rodney* (laid down May 1808) be built as quickly as possible; she was completed in some twenty months, a creditable achievement, but one which does not upstage the performance of John Barnard the Younger who, it will be recalled, in the Seven Years War, built and launched the ill-fated *Conqueror* in a little over a year. There was, however, a difference in size, the *Rodney* being a 74-gun ship of 1754 tons and the *Conqueror* a 70-gun ship of 1437 tons.

Table XVI
Naval vessels built 1805 -1813

Name	Rate	Guns	Ordered	Launched
Marlborough	3rd	74	31.1.1805	22.6.1807
Parthian	Brig Sloop	10	1807	13.2.1808
Rodney	3rd	74	28.5.1808	8.12.1809
Cornwall	3rd	74	13.7.1807	16.1.1812
Devonshire	3rd	74	28.5.1808	23.9.1812
Pactolus	5th	38	1812	14. 8.1813

East Indiaman *Asia*

The very last letter from Frances Barnard, Son and Roberts to the Navy Board was dated 30 June 1813. It was, in its own way, an historic document, for it brought to an end a correspondence carried on by three generations of the Barnard family, lasting some seventy two years, the first letter being dated 14 July 1740.

The letter is typical of the hundreds of letters dispatched to the Board by the Barnard family during their years of association, and as fitting end to the correspondence it is reproduced in full:

"Deptford Green, 30 June 1813.
Honourable Sirs
We beg leave to inform you the *Pactolus* of 38 guns building by us for His Majesty's Service is in such a state of forwardness as to enable us to launch her on the 14th August if it meets with the approbation of your Honoured Board. We hope Your Honours will be so kind as to order us to be supplied with the launching gear from His Majesty's Yard at Deptford. We remain.

Your most obedient Servants
Frances Barnard Son and Roberts."

Endorsed."Desire they will launch her on the day proposed as she is in all respects ready. Direct the officers to receive her and to supply launching gear." [91]

The defeat of Napoleon at Waterloo in 1815 brought in its train its own special problems, for the Admiralty found itself with a vast fleet on its hands for which there was little or no prospect of gainful employment. The repercussions of the situation quickly became apparent; for the flow of naval contracts, which the merchant builders had enjoyed over three quarters of a century, came to an abrupt end. Never again, in the life of the fighting wooden sailing ship, would the Navy Board require the building capacity of the merchant yards.

The acquisition of the Rotherhithe Yard, with its shipbuilding as well as its mast making facilities, allowed Frances Barnard, Son and Roberts to continue to build consecutively for both the Navy Board and the shipping interests of the H.E.I.C. With regard to the latter it is recorded that the mast making yard supplied masts and spars to the Company's Precedences in Bengal, Madras and Bombay: whether they were the sole suppliers is not known [92]. To all intent and purpose the shipbuilding section of the Rotherhithe Yard became an extension of the Deptford Green Yard, new orders, whether naval or East Indiamen, being allotted according to the space available. It must, nevertheless, be borne in mind that the Rotherhithe Yard was the private freehold of Edward George and, as such, he leased the shipbuilding facilities of the yard to Frances Barnard, Son and Roberts at an annual rent of three hundred and twenty two pounds per annum.

Although there was a short break in orders received following the death of William (II), the business of building East Indiamen continued.

Table XVI
East Indiamen built 1808-1825

Date	Name	Tons (approx.)	Husband	Voyages
1808	*Princess Amelia II*	1300	Robert Williams	10
1811	*Asia*	950	Henry Bonham	10
1811	*Prince Regent*	1000	"	10
1812	*Marquis of Wellington*	950	"	9
1815	*Blucher*	x	x	9
1815	*Wellington* (hoy)	69	x	9
1817	*Thos Coutts*	1300	Sir Robert Preston	8
1817	*Dunira*	1300	Geo. Palmer	8
1818	*Windsor*	1300	Felix Clay	7
1819	*Thames II*	1300	Abel Chapman	7
1820	*Hythe*	1300	Stewart Majorbanks	6
1825	*Lord Lowther*	1300	Henry Blanchard	4

The above mentioned ships were the last built by the Barnard family, and their building brought to an end years of dedicated endeavour. The circumstances which caused the family's withdrawal from the industry were partly the result of the bleak outlook for the shipbuilding industry and partly the human element in the personality and character of Edward George.

The outlook was indeed poor, for in addition to the aforementioned loss of naval contracts, the decision by Lord Liverpool's government in 1813 to put an end to the H.E.I.C.'s monopoly of trade with India, together with the introduction, in 1814, of the India Shipping Bill, posed a further threat to the prosperity of the River shipbuilder. Two letters, signed by a consortium of the said shipbuilders, addressed firstly to the Chancellor of the Exchequer, the Rt Hon Vansittart, dated 18 January 1814, and secondly to the Prime Minister, the Rt Hon Earl of Liverpool, dated 30 June 1814, set out the fears of the shipbuilders and include a plea for government protection. Both letters are given, in full:

LETTER 1.

"Crosby Square
Jan 18th 1814

Sir,

As we conclude the regulations respecting East India built shipping shortly to be submitted to Parliament are now under the consideration of Her Majesty's Ministers we cannot refrain from briefly expressing our hopes to you as Chancellor of the Exchequer and under whose peculiar care the protection of the Revenue necessarily devolves that a contravening or equalising Duty may form a part of the proposed Bill, thereby affording us that protection which the present depressed state of shipbuilders throughout the Kingdom, so imperatively calls for as it embraces not only the welfare of the important manufacture, but what is more essential, that of the Revenue and landed interests of the Country.

We the more earnestly pray for this increase from the circumstances of similar protection having been granted to the manufacturers of cotton, muslins, calicos, silks etc. in this country by the heavy Duties so judiciously imposed in their importation in a wrought state, amounting nearly to prohibition, it is to be hoped that a class of merchandise so material to a maritime state as shipwrights etc. avowedly will not be entirely overlooked.

It would be trespassing too much now to detail the many important arguments which present themselves in support of the assistance we solicit, we may however be permitted to refer you to letters we had the honour of addressing to my Lords Liverpool, Buckingham and Castlereagh on the 18th May last in which some of the principal bearings of the vital question are fully stated as well as in the accompanying schedule, to which we respectively beg leave to call your attention.

Representing other persons residing in various distant parts of the kingdom will, we trust, sufficiently apologise for your anxiety to be informed as early as possible of the nature of the regulations proposed on this most important measure to enable us to communicate with them and possibly thereby prevent our giving unnecessary trouble to H.M.Government, a circumstance we are most anxious to avoid at the present eventful crisis.

Relying with confidence on the disposition so constantly evinced by H.M.Government to protect the Revenues and to impose, extend and foster the trade of the Empire, on the wisdom of Parliament and the justice of our present application for Legislative interference.

We have the honour to be
Sir
Your most humble servants

Wells Wigram and Green
Danl. and Saml Brent and Sons
Frances Barnard, Son and Roberts
Peter E. Graton

Rt.Honbl. Vansittart   Curling Cox and Co.
Chancellor of the Exchequer   Almon Hill and Sons." [93]

LETTER 2.

"Duke St.Westminster
30th June 1814

My Lord

We beg to request the favour of your perusal of the enclosed papers before the second reading of the India Shipping Bill in the House of Commons on Monday next in the hope that his Majesty's Government will be induced to afford us and their English Shipbuilders the protection we have most respectfully solicited of them

We are my Lord

Your faithful Hbl Servt
E.G.Barnard
William Pitcher
Daniel Brent
William Curling Jnr.
James Hill

The Right Honourable The Lord Liverpool" [94].

It was, indeed, a cruel quirk of fate that the proposed legislation should be introduced at a moment when the merchant shipbuilders were about to suffer the complete and utter loss of Navy Board contracts, but notwithstanding the seemingly abysmal outlook for the industry the majority of the signatories to the two letters managed to survive until the coming of iron and steam. The Barnard family being a noted exception.

Edward George's decision to withdraw from the industry was a matter of personal choice not necessarily based solely on economic considerations. A study of his life indicates that he was a different calibre of man from his brother, father and forebears, all of whom had been practical hard working men blessed with foresight and business acumen. His own inclinations would seem to have led him to administration rather than management – a committee man rather than a man of business.

He was certainly a scrupulously honest man with strict principles. He had an eye to his rights and was a painstaking worker. He was possibly ahead of his time in that he had a social conscience – a fact which eventually led him into the political arena. Excellent though these qualities may have been, he unfortunately lacked the will, drive and imagination to pilot the business through the difficulties of the period.

It must be emphasised that the demise of the shipbuilding interests was not a cut and dried affair, for the businesses were neither officially wound up nor were the leases sold; the businesses themselves simply withered and died over a period of years.

It must be said to his credit, however, that for a time he had struggled to keep the businesses afloat, for in 1819 he decided to renew and enlarge the gates of the dry dock of the Rotherhithe Yard and in so doing became involved in a bureaucratic tussle with the Worshipful Committee for Improving the Navigation on the River Thames [95]. His application underwent procedures not uncommon today in planning circles; for it was passed up and down from committee to committee, outline and detailed plans had to be drawn-up, a site-inspection team was appointed and the Water Bailiff and the Clerk of the Works had to be consulted. After many months the application was rubber-stamped by the Grand Committee on payment of a fee of ten guineas. Subsequent minutes, recorded some three years later suggest that the work was never carried out.

In June 1823 a more serious matter arose which caused Edward George to enlist the help of the Bridge House Estates, who, it will be recalled, were landlords of the Deptford Green Yard. The matter in question was an application being considered by the aforementioned Worshipful Committee to allow an applicant to lay down moorings for five vessels for use as floating docks for the repair of shipping, two of which would be in the vicinity of the Rotherhithe Yard. The licence, if granted, had damaging implications for the river-side yards for, being free of taxes and rents, the newcomers would automatically have a competitive edge. The Bridge House Estates rigorously opposed the application on behalf of their tenants. Edward George submitted an eight page 'memorial' in which, among other considerations, he emphasised the fact that his docks at Deptford Green and Rotherhithe were already 'virtually shut' as a result of the depressed state of shipping, and that to grant a licence would deprive him 'of the little business which yet remains' [96]. Unfortunately the surviving minutes of the Worshipful Committee do not disclose the final outcome.

The end of the road 1825-51

In view of his statement in his 'memorial' that his yards were virtually shut it is not surprising that when a suitable opportunity occurred for him to follow his own inclinations he took it with alacrity. On 17 July 1825 Frances Barnard died at her home in Mitcham at the grand old age of eighty eight years and eleven months. Edward George had at long last become his own master and he wasted little time in moving to pastures new. In the same year that his mother died he

East Indiaman *Thos Coutts*

purchased Gosfield Hall, Essex, from the Duke of Buckingham for the sum of one hundred and fifty thousand pounds; it was a large mansion dating back to the reign of Queen Elizabeth, standing in two thousand acres of prime farmland. On 7 April 1827 he married Jamaican-born Eliza Millard at Gosfield Parish Church and in 1832 he entered politics, becoming one of the MPs for the new Parliamentary Division of Greenwich. A synopsis of his political life will be found in Appendix XV.

Notwithstanding his changed circumstances Edward George, was obliged to attend to matters of consequence which, from time to time, arose in respect of his shipbuilding interests. In 1834 for instance he was embroiled in a court case with the Deptford Green Council over the assessment of thirty four pounds seven shillings and six pence in respect of the local Poor Rate, which he declined to pay on a question of principle. He argued that he was being assessed on a part of a yard which had not been in use over the period of assessment and that rates were payable on the occupation of and not merely on the holding of the premises, a point of view strongly opposed by the solicitor acting for the Parish. Evidence given disclosed that the yard had been empty for some nine months, and when asked whether he objected to the whole or only part of the assessment he replied that he objected to the whole, and that in principle he wished for relief in accordance with occupation. The Board of Magistrates found in favour of the Parish. The case caused a considerable stir in the Parish for it was indeed a novel experience to have the local Member of Parliament charged with the non-payment of Rates - especially of the Poor Rate. A considerable amount of ill feeling was engendered in the locality, bringing in its train a bitter pamphleteering war between the parties involved.

Whilst the hearing was in progress, part of the yard, probably the dry dock, was occupied by the East Indiaman *Thos Coutts*, launched by Frances Barnard Son and Roberts some seventeen years earlier in 1817; she was in for cleaning and repairs after completing her eighth voyage to the east. A newspaper report of 8 November 1834 expressed the hope "that the Parish will devise an increased bustle from the employment of the necessary hands engaged upon her." There are no further reports of the yard again being used for servicing vessels of a similar nature.

The very last references which have been traced of the Barnard family's yards on the River are to be found in the minutes of the aforementioned Worshipful Committee. The first, in September 1840, concerned

A vessel undergoing breaming (cleaning off a ship's bottom by fire) at Rotherhithe in a hulk used as a dry dock

danger emanating from a waterfront obstruction in the form of an old slipway of the Rotherhithe Yard; the second, recorded some ten years later in 1850, was a similar complaint lodged in respect of an obstruction at the Deptford Green Yard. There is no evidence of the steps taken by Edward George to mitigate the dangers of which the river users complained. It would appear from the available evidence that the yards were, for all practical purposes, abandoned in the late 1830's.

Edward George died suddenly at Gosfield Hall, on 14 June 1851 at seventy three years of age, and was buried in the family vault at Gosfield Church. His death brought to an end the Barnard family's age-long commitment to shipbuilding. His final years and the problems he left behind were a sorry and unedifying end to the family's fortunes. It must be admitted that the tide of economic circumstances had flowed strongly against him, but no matter how the situation in which he found himself may be rationalised, the impression remains that he was the wrong man, in the wrong place at the wrong time.

His will had been drawn up in November 1832 and showed him to have been a man of very considerable wealth. It was a document of great length and complexity, which set up various family trusts and made a large number of generous bequests to friends and relations. His wife, Eliza, was appointed sole executrix and residuary legatee. It was proved on 18 May 1852 but, at a later date, the list of legatees held by the Inland Revenue was marked 'Insolvent'.

The death of Edward George exposed a financial situation of extreme gravity; for it revealed that in order to support his chosen way of life he had borrowed to a state of insolvency. The amount of his borrowing is not known, but evidence has survived which shows that, as early as 1832, he obtained a twenty five thousand pounds loan by mortgaging part of the estate. Further mortgages were taken out in subsequent years with the result that, on his death, the estate had to be sold in order to satisfy his creditors.

The humiliation suffered by his wife and children at having to dispose of such a grand family home must have been traumatic in the extreme, and is probably reflected in the fact that his wife Eliza, died only three years later at approximately sixty eight years of age, and that his only son Edward George, for a short period of his adult life, became mentally disturbed (see Addendum).

Such a melancholy ending could well detract from the achievements of previous generations, whose dedication and drive had ensured the growth and prosperity of the business. In order to put the matter into perspective a summary of the very positive achievements of the Barnard family in the field of shipbuilding between the years c.1739 and 1825 shows that operating either on their own account, or in partnership, members of the family built a minimum of 144 vessels in their yards at Ipswich, Harwich and on the River Thames; of this total seventy eight were naval vessels ranging from sloops to 3rd rates of 74 guns. Barnard built vessels were engaged in major battles such as The Glorious First June, the Nile, and Trafalgar. Statistics show that between the years 1739-1815 the Barnard Yards built more ships-of-the-line than any other merchant builder in the country. The number of vessels taken in for repair and refitting has not been recorded. In the field of merchant shipping the family constructed sixty two East Indiamen and four smaller vessels for the shipping interests of the H.E.I.C. In addition, a limited number of contracts would have been executed for other parties whose records have not survived.

In conclusion, it may be fairly claimed that, together with other merchant builders similarly placed, the Barnard Yards made a major contribution to this country's maritime achievements from the first half of the eighteenth century up to the Battle of Trafalgar in 1805, when the Royal Navy established a supremacy at sea which remained unchallenged for a hundred years.

Gosfield Hall, Halstead, Essex
(*Reproduced by courtesy of the Essex Record Office*)

Gosfield Hall, north front
(*Reproduced by courtesy of the Essex Record Office*)

Epilogue

The catastrophic state of the family's financial affairs must not only have come as a great shock to the widow Eliza but must also have been extremely distressing; for the Hall had been her home since her marriage in 1827 and both her children had been born within its walls. To find herself suddenly homeless and, to all intent and purpose, penniless, with two adult children, was an emotional blow from which she and the children possibly never fully recovered.

The upkeep of a property of the size and age of Gosfield Hall (Appendix XVI) imposed a heavy burden on an owner; for it contained approximately one hundred rooms and was said to have a window for each day of the year. The number of staff required to run and maintain such an establishment was considerable, and there can be little doubt the financial pressure forced Edward George to reduce the level of staff to a minimum; but he retained a sufficient number to attend to the immediate needs of the family. Such a policy resulted in parts of the Hall, probably the State Rooms, falling into a sorry state of disrepair.

On the other hand the farms were well managed and produced an income of some £4,000 to £5,000 per annum. The words of Mr James Beadle, the auctioneer who presided over the sale of the estate held at the Auction Market, Bartholomew Lane, London, on 13 November 1851, give a clear and concise account of their well-being. In his introduction he said:

"It (the Hall) was situated in a great county, was richly timbered and in the heart of one of the most picturesque and fertile parts of Essex. Its farms were numerous, productive, and in good preservation....With regard to the site, he was of the opinion that it was one of the best districts in the County of Essex. The land was now well drained, and their farmers could compete with any farmer or agriculturists in the kingdom... The late proprietor, as was well known, was particularly fond of farming, and had been most successful in such agreeable pursuit. He had been awarded several prizes, and so productive was the soil that he could have let every acre of the land if the solicitor of the mortgagees had authorised him so to do...it was rarely indeed that an estate was to be found upon which the farm-houses were in such a thorough state of repairs as those of the Gosfield Hall Estate."

In 1854 the estate was bought by Mr Samuel Courtauld, head of the well known family of textile manufacturers, who not only returned the Hall to its former glory but also made significant improvements. On his death in 1881 the property passed to his adopted daughter, Mrs Lowe. In common with many similar properties the Hall was taken over by the military during the course of World War II, after which, unoccupied and with the ground derelict and overgrown, it fell into such a state of dilapidation that demolition was threatened. It was saved by the Essex County Council, who purchased it on account of its outstanding historical associations. It was later sold to the Wayfarers Trust Ltd who in turn sold it to its present owner The Country Homes Association.

Eliza Barnard, the widow of Edward George, only survived her husband by some three years. She died on 27 June 1854 at the Greenwich home of her unmarried sister-in-law Frances Barnard; she was sixty eight years of age. It is not without interest that she died in the same year that the Hall was sold to Samuel Courtauld.

The deaths of Edward George and of his wife Eliza would seem a fitting end to this history except for the fact that the male line, in the person of Edward George Jnr. lingered on until the closing years of the century. He was, by any standard, a strange man, subject to extraordinary bouts of irrational behaviour which may well have had its roots in the shock he received when, on the threshold of manhood, he lost both his parents and the estate to which he was heir. A brief outline of his life and the fantasies he suffered will be found in the addendum.

Addendum

Edward George (II)

Edward George was born in December 1831; he matriculated from Oxford University in 1851. His father died insolvent later in the same year and his mother died some three years later in 1854. In 1861 he was living with his aunt, Frances Barnard, in Greenwich and was employed as a clerk in a government office. His aunt died in 1863 aged 89 years. A codicil to her will, dated 20 August 1861, revoked Edward George as one of her executors, but at the same time confirmed the bequests she had bestowed in his favour, which were, in essence, half her estate. Whether his removal as an executor had any connection with an instability which surfaced in 1873 is a matter for conjecture.

His bizarre behaviour may indicate that he suffered from a form of schizophrenia which, in 1873, caused him to experience illusions of grandeur for in the spring of that year he wrote to Queen Victoria suggesting that she should grant him a peerage because of certain important connections he believed were enjoyed by his mother's mother. The letter was passed to Sir Thomas Biddulph, who replied that Her Majesty could only grant such a request on the recommendation of the Prime Minister - Mr Gladstone. Greatly encouraged by this information, Edward George wrote immediately to the Prime Minister, as under:

> "Portland Chambers
> Gt. Titchfield St.W.
> June 4 1873
>
> Sir,
> Having made a request to the Queen that Her Majesty would confer a Peerage upon me in consideration of rank to which I may be entitled in right of my Mother but of which I do not myself possess the proof. Sir Thomas Biddulph's answer was to the effect that the Queen could not grant my request except at your recommendation.
> Sir Thomas made use of the expression "upon claim to a peerage" which was rather a misinterpretation of the meaning of my letter, for if I preferred any definite claim the proper course would naturally be to bring it before the House of Lords in the usual manner - I wish therefore distinctly to state that it is not my actual claim which I urge, but a request that Her Majesty will graciously please to grant a Peerage for the above mentioned reason.
> My Father's long services to the Whig Government as Member for Greenwich could not certainly entitle me to expect an Honour, though Baronetcies have frequently been given for life but still I hope that they may be taken into consideration with reference to which I request in right of my mother.
> The portrait of my Mother's Mother, of which I enclose a photograph for your acceptance, has been taken by many people to be that of some one of importance and during your visit to His Grace The Duke of Devonshire, to whom I have already sent a copy, may perhaps be regarded with sufficient interest to require further investigation for many people now living believe that my Mother's Mother was an Heiress of importance though I am not at present able to prove it.
> I cannot express myself further on the subject than to say that I throw myself on the liberality of Her Majesty's Government.
>
> I have the honour to be
> Sir
> Your most obedient Servant
> E.George Barnard.
> W.E.Gladstone" [97].

There is no record of Mr Gladstone's reply but, not surprisingly, Edward George remained a plain 'mister'.

The second incident occurred in September 1873, the action moving to the Gosfield Estate and to the Court of the local magistrates. It had far more serious undertones than the affair of the peerage.

On 1 September 1873 Mr Samuel Courtauld, who it will be recalled had purchased the estate in 1854, received the following unsigned telegram:

> "From a friend to Samuel Courtauld Esq., Gosfield Hall, near Halstead, Essex. The heir of Gosfield is coming to shoot over the estate tomorrow, so prepare to meet him. His licence is already taken out, so no doubt he means mischief. Be careful what you do, I fear the consequences."

The background to this extraordinary communication was that for some time past Edward George had periodically trespassed on the estate claiming that, as the appointed heir, he was the rightful owner. In pursuance of this idea he persisted in his right to shoot over the estate as and when he pleased.

It would appear that until the arrival of the said telegram Mr Courtauld had treated the affair with considerable patience; but its implied threat of violence caused him to report the matter to the police. Edward George was, thereupon, apprehended and duly charged with threatening behaviour and brought before the local magistrates.

In evidence Mr Courtauld stated that he believed there was a danger that the defendant would attack him if he attempted to restrain him from shooting on the estate. He believed that any interference would be at the peril of his life.

The defendant denied using any threat or of entertaining any personal feeling against Mr Courtauld, but believing himself to be the heir to the estate he had the right to shoot over it at his pleasure. He admitted being the writer of the letter. The case was adjourned.

The adjournment caused Edward George further difficulties, for he was unable to find sureties for bail although he approached everybody in the Courtroom, from the magistrates down. On the suggestion of Mr Courtauld, bail was reduced from £200 to £100 but still no surety was forthcoming. The accused was duly placed in custody.

The Braintree and Bocking Advertiser of 10 September, reporting the case, had this to say about the demeanour of the defendant in court:

" (he) appeared keenly to feel his position...his request that he might be allowed to remain at an hotel for the night being very properly refused.... Throughout the examination Mr Barnard conducted himself in a quiet and gentlemanly manner and tendered his apologies to Mr Courtauld and his assurance that he intended him no harm, a frankness which certainly carried conviction to the minds of those present."

The following week the same newspaper reported that as Edward George was about to be moved to Springfield Gaol he wrote to Mr Courtauld as follows:

"As I have already stated to other gentlemen in the neighbourhood I will give you my word of honour that I will leave the neighbourhood tomorrow and will not henceforth trespass upon the Gosfield Hall Estate."

Mr Courtauld replied that he would rely upon Mr Barnard's good faith, and thereupon took the necessary measures to secure Mr Barnard's release, which was effected the same afternoon. There is no evidence that he, the young man, broke his word.

On 30 March 1882, Edward George married Stephana Walker, daughter of George Walker, barrister, at St Marylebone Church, London. He died some fifteen years later at 88 Maison Dieu Rd, Dover, at sixty five years of age – there were no children of the marriage. His occupation on his death certificate was given as 'Independent Landed Proprietor'.

Appendices

I   Aprenticeship indenture of Henry Barnard to Alexander Cubitt, enrolled at Great Yarmouth, 7 May 1591

II   The Barnard family of Shipwrights of Lowestoft

III   John Barnard the Elder

IV   The last Will and testament of John Barnard the Elder, 25 Dec. 1716

V   The Dissenter's Meeting House, Tacket St, Ipswich

VI   John Barnard, High Sheriff of the County of Suffolk, 1766

VII   Sundry Navy Bill receipts and the discounts charged thereon as per the statement of John Barnard with Alexander's Bank, Ipswich from 19 March 1779 to 19 March 1780

VIII Analysis of the list of creditors of John Barnard who were paid ten shillings in the pound in the years 1785-6. The balance of ten shillings being paid in January 1789

IX   The *Pandora*

X   An account of a Method for the safe Removal of Ships that have been driven on Shore, and damaged their Bottoms, to places (however distant) for repairing them

XI   The Deptford Green Yard. Leases taken by William Barnard 1780-87 from the Bridge House Estates

XII   "Success to Mr Barnard's Yard." Inscription on a Chinese Export Porcelain Presentation Punch Bowl

XIII Frances Barnard c.1736-1825

XIV The *Warren Hastings* and *La Piémontaise*

XV   Edward George Barnard, politician 1832-1851

XVI Gosfield Hall

XVII Ship Lists - Naval Vessels and East Indiamen

XVIII The wreck of the East Indiaman *Winterton*

Appendix I

Apprenticeship indenture of Henry Barnard to Alexander Cubitt, enrolled at Great Yarmouth, 17th May 1591

[Latin]

MEMORANDUM, that on the seventeenth day of May in the thirty third year of the reign of our lady Elizabeth, by the grace of God Queen of England, France and Ireland, Defender of the Faith, etc. [17th May 1591] Alexander Cubitt came before Ralph Wolhouse and John Harrys, Bailiffs of the Borough and Town of Great Yarmouth in the County of Norfolk, and produced a certain indenture and asked for it to be enrolled according to the ancient and laudable custom of the aforesaid town; and it is enrolled, in these words:

[English]

THIS INDENTURE MADE the seventeenth day of May in the three and thirty year of the reign of Elizabeth, by the grace of God Queen of England, France and Ireland, Defender of the Faith etc., between Alexander Cubitt of Great Yarmouth in the County of Norfolk, Shipwright, of the one part, and Henry Barnard, the son of William Barnard late of Lowestoft in the County of Suffolk, Shipwright, deceased, of the other part, witnesseth that the said Henry, of his own motion and free will, and by the consent of his friends, hath put himself an apprentice unto the said Alexander, unto his said occupation of shipwright's craft to be learned, and after the manner of an apprentice with him to dwell, tarry, serve and abide, from the feast of Pentecost next coming after the date hereof [23 May 1591] until the full end and term of nine years from thence next ensuing and fully to be complete, ended and determined; during all which term the said Henry granteth by these presents the said Alexander as his Master, well and truly to serve. His secrets he shall keep; his commandments, lawfull and honest, everywhere he shall do, no fornication during the said term he shall commit, under pain of doubling of his said term; hurt unto his Master he shall none do, nor of any other consent be done, but he to his power shall it let, or anon his said Master thereof warn, taverns of custom he shall not frequent, except it be about the business of his said Master there to be done; at the dice, cards or any other unlawful games prohibited by the law he shall not play; the goods of his said Master inordinately he shall not waste, not them to any person lend without the consent of his said Master; matrimony within the said term he shall not contract, not espouse, not from his said service neither by day not yet by night he shall absent or prolong himself; but as a true and faithful servant ought to do he shall behave himself honestly, as well in word as in deed during all the said term.

AND the said Alexander Cubitt covenanteth and granteth to and with the said Henry Barnard by these presents that he, the said Alexander, shall teach and inform, or cause to be taught and informed, the said Henry in his said occupation of Shipwright's craft after the best manner that he can or may, according to the capacity of the said Henry, and duly and honestly him to chastise, finding unto the said apprentice sufficient meat, drink, lodging and apparel during all the said term; and also in the end of the said term to give and deliver, or cause to be delivered, unto the said Henry, as well an axe, and adze, a handsaw, an auger a caulking iron, a pair of clink hammers, a clove hammer, and a mallet, as also double apparel to and for his body, meet and convenient, viz. apparel for holidays and apparel for working days.

IN WITNESS whereof here unto these present indentures the said parties have set their seals interchangeably. Given the day and year first above mentioned [98].

Appendix II

The Barnard family of Shipwrights of Lowestoft

Surviving records reveal that four members of three generations of the Barnard family resident in Lowestoft were shipwrights, their years of service covering a period of approximately one hundred years.

In 1524 a Robert Bernard (later given as Barnard) paid a lay subsidy of one shilling on movable goods assessed at one pound, his occupation is not recorded. Robert had two sons Wyllyam and Robert. The elder son Wyllyam became a shipwright about the year 1560 and his son Henry, born 15 June 1577, is the Henry whose apprenticeship indenture is given in Appendix I. Wyllyam died 21 June 1580.

The younger son of Robert Bernard, Robert junior, became a carpenter and owned a yard which probably had a frontage close to or abutting the then coastline. His son Thomas, born 21 January 1575, served his apprenticeship at about the same time as his cousin Henry. Thomas married in 1602 and his son Symon, born 28 October 1610, followed his father into the shipwright's trade probably between the years 1620-30.

Symon married in 1635 and it is of interest that his younger son John, was baptised in the Parish of Southwold on 31 May 1644. It would appear that the family had moved from Lowestoft as no further entries relating to the family appear in the Lowestoft records.

No link has so far been made between the Lowestoft and Ipswich families.

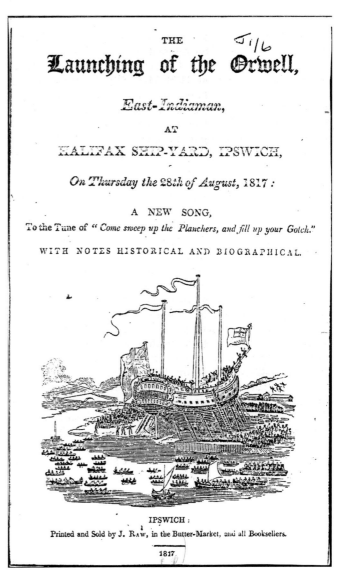

Front cover of song-sheet celebrating the launching of the East Indiaman *Orwell*

Appendix III

John Barnard the Elder

Here Resteth in Hope
Mr John Barnard
Shipwright
who departed this life
the 18th January 1717
Aged 52 years
Likewise Mary his wife
who departed this life
the....of March 1732
Aged 66 years

The above is reported to have been inscribed on a memorial tablet erected in the churchyard of the Parish Church of St Clements, Ipswich, all trace of which has been lost. It was doubtless commissioned by John Barnard the Younger in memory of his parents. The statement that John Barnard the Elder was fifty two years of age at his time of death is the only known evidence which allows a calculation to be made of his date of birth.

A record of the memorial is to be found in a contemporary song sheet with the title "The launching of the *Orwell*, East Indiaman at the Halifax Shipyard, Ipswich". It was sung to the tune of "Come sweep up the Planchers and fill your Gotch" and was published in Ipswich in 1817. The publication contains a large number of historical and biographical notes many of which are grossly inaccurate.

Appendix IV

The last Will and testament of John Barnard the Elder, 25 Dec. 1716 [99]

Memorandum, I John Barnard of Ipswich in the County of Suffolk, shipwright, being sick and weak in body but of sound disposing mind and memory do make and ordain this my last Will and testament made this twenty fifth day of December in the year of our Lord one thousand seven hundred and sixteen and in the third year of the reign of our Sovereign Lord George by the Grace of God King of Great Britain, France and Ireland. Imprinis I give and devise unto Mary my loving wife all that my house, messuages, and tenements wherein I now dwell together with all their appurtenances and also all that my lands and yards commonly called the dock-yards together with the wharf, launch, dock, key, and all other the appurtenances thereto belonging which I lately purchased of Thomasin Blomfield and Mary Hubbard as the said house and dockyard with their and every of their appurtenances situate and lying and being in the Parish of St Clements in Ipswich aforesaid. To hold all the said Messuages, tenements, lands, and premises unto her the said Mary and to her heirs for ever. Item, I will that all my just debts be paid and satisfied and I give and bequeth unto my said loving wife full and sole executrix of this my said will and testement hereby revoking all other Wills by me made or caused to be made and having heard that my Will be deliberately read over to approve the same and every part thereof and do publish and declare this to be my last Will and testement in the presence of those witnesses that have hereto subscribed their names in witness whereof I have hereunto set my hand and seal the day and year above.

Signed and sealed John Barnard
Signed sealed published and declared by the said John Barnard the testator to be his last Will and testement in the presence of us who have subscribed our names as witnesses in the presence of the testator
Elizabeth Beardwell
James Cole
Will Clarke

Appendix V

The Dissenter's Meeting House, Tacket St, Ipswich

John the Elder and his wife Mary were members of a sect of Dissenters which had been established in Green Yard in the Parish of St Peter, Ipswich in 1686. The sect prospered and it became necessary to obtain larger premises. In 1718 the congregation purchased a freehold in Tacket St (then Tankard St) on which they erected a new chapel. Worship commenced in the year 1720.

In a paper written some 170 years later by Thomas Conder under the heading "Recollections of a Deacon 1894" [100], he claimed that John Barnard the Younger played a leading role in both the funding and in the construction of the new chapel. However, bearing in mind that the recollections of the writer were based on the recollections of his grandmother (Deborah Conder nee Barnard), who was not born until some 26 years after the events in question had occurred, it would be hardly surprising if the memories of both parties had become blurred.

The account claims that as well as contributing to the funding, John the Younger also provided men from his shipyard to assist with the building, and that, in addition, he provided two large masts from a man o'war to act as pillars for supporting the roof. He is also credited with providing the Trustees with a handsome chandelier, costing one hundred pounds, which hung in the body of the chapel for many years.

It is probable that the Barnard family did make a substantial contribution to the project by one means or another but, as John the Younger (b.1705) would only have been fifteen years of age at the time and still serving his apprenticeship under William Gooday, it is doubtful whether he could have been the prime mover and thereby played the role allotted him. An educated guess would suggest that credit should be given to his mother Mary, widowed in 1717, who, so it would appear, took over the reins of the yard on her husband's death.

The Old Chapel, Tacket Street. The entrance and the minister's house

Appendix VI

John Barnard, High Sheriff of the County of Suffolk, 1766

Deborah Conder (1746-1825) neé Barnard. Daughter of John Barnard the Younger Married John Conder 1768 Source: Suffolk Record Office PR/C/28

The appointment of John Barnard as Sheriff of the County of Suffolk is something of an enigma as his name does not appear on the List of Sheriffs held by the Office of the Sheriff of Suffolk, however, there are a number of references to his holding such a post, the most reliable of which is to be found in a letter written by the Rev David Edwards, minister of Tacket St Chapel to the Rev Dr Conder, Principal of Homerton College, London, dated 12 April 1766 [101].

The letter contains a detailed description of the public hanging of two young men convicted of the theft of one hundred pounds which had taken place two days earlier on Rushmoor Heath, near Ipswich. Prior to their execution the condemned men asked to attend a service at the Tacket St Chapel, a request which had to be sanctioned by the Sheriff of the County, the relevant passage reads:

"...he (the Minister) went to meet Mr Peter Clarke (Solicitor) and Deputy Sheriff of the County to obtain his permission and the permission of Mr Barnard, Sheriff of the County who resided in St Clement's Parish, Shipbuilder."

Permission was duly granted.

Appendix VII

Sundry Navy Bill receipts and the discounts charged thereon as per the statement of John Barnard with Alexander's Bank, Ipswich from 19 March 1779 to 19 March 1780

19 March 1779	By Navy Bill	£4011.18. 0	
	Less discount $7\frac{1}{2}$%	300.17.11	
	Less Commission	5. 0. 4	
		£3705.19. 9	Net credit

26 March	By Navy Bill	£2929.10. 0	
	Less discount 7 %	208.14. 6	
	Less Commission	3.13. 3	
		£2717. 2. 3	Net credit

5 April 1779	By Navy Bill	£ 978. 4. 0	
	Less discount 8%	78. 5. 6	
	Less Commission	1. 4. 6	
		£ 898.14. 0	Net credit

29 May	By Navy Bill	£1351. 4. 0	
	Less discount 7 %	106. 8. 2	
	Less Commission	1.13.10	
		£1243. 2. 0	Net credit

6 July	By Navy Bill	£2260.00. 0	
	Less discount $10\frac{1}{2}$%	238. 2. 9	
	Less Commission	2.16. 9	
		£2027.00. 6	Net credit

19 March 1780	By Navy Bill	£3805.00. 0	
	Less discount $11\frac{1}{4}$%	428. 1. 3	
	Less Commission	4.16. 3	
		£3372. 2. 6	Net credit

Bills received after this date were credited after the deduction of both the discount and of commission charged and thereby omitted the rate of the discount levied [102].

Appendix VIII

Analysis of the list of creditors of John Barnard who were paid ten shillings in the pound in the years 1785-6. The balance of ten shillings being paid in January 1789

The total amount of the indebtedness amounted to £6304. 3. 3.
The list shows that the number of creditors totalled 105, the majority of whom were owed less than £20 each.

Over £200		£100-£200	
John Abbott	£236. 5. 8	Wm Hammond	£141.17. 6
S.R.Smith	231. 3.00	H.Nunns	104.15. 0
Owen & Collet	272.10.00	T.Fenn	150.18. 7
		J.Ashley	194.13. 5
		Till & Death	165.00. 0
		J.Forsett	120. 7. 3
		W.Summers	103. 3. 6
		Geo.Notcutt	130. 5. 4

£50-£100		£20-£50	
Wm Janold	£ 81.00.10	I.Gage	£ 25. 1. 7
R.Tiffin	50.00.10	D.Cracknell	26.17. 9
J.Bird	57.12. 4	J.Hill	34. 7. 6
P.Hart	84.19.00	W.Borwick	20.00. 0
S.Teague	80. 4. 4	W.Strutt	26. 6. 7
Corp.of Harwich	65.11. 6	R.Ellerby	41. 5. 0
J.Webber	60.18. 9	D.Bowell	42.12. 0
M.Parkes	53. 1. 3	J.Syer	40.15. 5

12/- to £20

In this category there are 78 names of which 27 were owed less than £5 each. The first 10/- repayments were staggered, commencing on 31st August 1785 and ending 4th March 1786. Details of the 1789 payments have been lost.

Appendix IX

The *Pandora*

The Mutiny on the *Bounty* and the subsequent adventures and suffering of Lt William Bligh and his eighteen crewmen, set adrift in a 23ft. open boat in the far Pacific by master's-mate Fletcher Christian, is one of the best known stories in maritime history. Their forty-one day journey of 3600 miles to the VOC settlement of Coupmang on the island of Timor has been the subject of a number of films.

The equally exciting and dramatic story of the frigate *Pandora* has received little publicity in the northern hemisphere, although in Australia, in maritime circles, she is regarded in much the same way as the *Mary Rose* in this country. In the year 1790 the Admiralty issued the following instructions to Capt Edwards, commander of the *Pandora*:

"whereas the ship you command has been fitted out for the express purpose of proceeding to the South Seas in order to ....recover the Armed Vessel *Bounty* and to bring in confinement to England Fletcher Christian and his associates ....you are hereby and directed to put to sea and proceed as expeditiously as possible to the South Seas and shape your course around Cape Horn and steer for Matavai Bay ....on the Northside of Tahiti." [103]

The *Pandora* sailed from Portsmouth on 7 November 1790 with a compliment of 132 men. Her four ship's boats - cutters - had been replaced by yawls. She arrived at Matavai Bay, via Tenerife, Rio de Janerio and Cape Horn, on 23 March 1791. Four of the *Bounty* men instantly came aboard and surrendered; next day three more followed suit. Within a week fourteen mutineers were retaken. Fletcher Christian, together with eight associates, was then living on Pitcairn Island. It was a quirk of fate that, on the voyage from Cape Horn to Tahiti, Capt Edwards, in the *Pandora*, missed Pitcairn by only a day's sail. A four month's search over a wide area failed to find the nine missing men. In early August 1791 Capt Edwards turned for home and on 26th of that month the *Pandora* was in sight of the Barrier Reef off the Murray Islands. Seeking a passage through the dangerous and uncharted waters of the Torres Straits the *Pandora* struck an isolated outcrop of submerged reef. She had grounded close to lowtide but, as the tide changed she beat over the reef and anchored in relatively sheltered water. Unhappily the damage to her hull in the course of her grounding proved irreparable and she eventually sank in seventeen fathoms. Thirty crew members and four Bounty prisoners drowned. The survivors, eighty nine crew and ten prisoners, in the four ships boats, found refuge on a conveniently adjacent sand cay. Stranded as he was, with no hope of rescue, Capt Edwards had little option but to attempt to sail to the nearest centre of civilisation - the VOC settlement at Coupang on the island of Timor some 1100 miles distant. The crew had fortunately been able to salvage provisions from the stricken vessel. Three days were spent on the sand cay making preparations for the voyage. On a final visit to the *Pandora* the ship's cat was found clinging to the rigging. The party departed from the sand cay on 1 September 1791. Good progress was made through the Torres Strait and in twenty-four hours a landfall was made near Cape York where luckily fresh water was found. In eleven days the Arafura Sea was crossed and the men arrived at Coupang on 16 September 1791.

The Bounty mutineers were housed in a 'cage' which Capt Edwards, a strict disciplinarian, had ordered to be built on the *Pandora's* quarter-deck. Nicknamed 'Pandora's box' it was some 11ft in length with a width of 18ft, in the roof was a 20in. square trapdoor secured by a bar. The ankles of the mutineers were secured by bilboes and their wrists were manacled. Once in England, the prisoners faced a six day trial in September 1792. The courts martial sentenced six of the ten to hang but only three of the sentences were carried out, two of the six being pardoned and one discharged on a technicality. The remaining four were acquitted.

The wreck of the *Pandora* lay undisturbed for some 186 years. It was not until November 1977, using sophisticated equipment, including a RAAF Neptune aircraft, that her whereabouts was finally established. An archaeological assessment survey, carried out in 1979, rated the site, not only as a first class wreck, but one which was thought could prove to be the best preserved in Australian waters. The site was brought within the protection of the Australian Historic Shipwrecks Act which, off the Queensland coast, was administered by the Queensland Museum.

A first season of major excavation began in October 1983, the main object being to ascertain the orientation and exact extent of the buried hull and to collect a representative sample of ship's fittings, stores and crew's possessions. The season was encouraging in that 256 artefacts were recovered including a gold and silver fob watch, together with a large number of medical implements and other delicate items. Among the first of the weighty artefacts to be raised was one of the *Pandora's* twenty-four cannon. The season's work indicated that the *Pandora* was a rich storehouse and that further excavation would provide the largest collection of artefacts ever recovered from an eighteenth century shipwreck in Australian waters.

A second season commenced in November 1984. Two hundred and eighty-three artefacts were excavated. One being a complete fireplace from an officer's cabin and another the iron Brodie stove from the *Pandora's* galley. The predominant artefacts were ships fastenings, such as bolts and nails, and fittings, such as gunport hinges and glass window frames.

The third season, in 1986, saw the largest expedition mounted on the site and involved 37 divers, 17 ships crew and 20 operations staff. In all some 786 artefacts were recovered which ranged from navigational instruments, sand timers, crockery, wine glasses and part of a flint-lock pistol.

In 1994 the Queensland Museum put forward plans for a series of excavations aimed at completing the recovery of all artefacts by 2000-1. A major display was planned to coincide with the Olympic Games in Sydney in the year 2000. To assist with fund raising the Museum established a Foundation to raise some A$2 million. The sums raised would supplement the A$1 million subsidy provided by the Queensland Government.

Some medical equipment attributed to Surgeon George Hamilton

Sand time bottles

A finial, probably from an andiron leg, an accessory on the Great Cabin fireplace

Appendix X

An account of a Method for the safe Removal of Ships that have been driven on Shore, and damaged their Bottoms, to places (however distant) for repairing them

By Mr William Barnard, Shipbuilder, Grove St, Deptford. A paper read to the Royal Society by the Astronomer Royal,

Nevil Maskelyne DD. FRS., on 23rd December 1779.

Deptford, April 14, 1779.

On the shores of this island, distinguished for its formidable fleets and extensive commerce, and so particularly situated, there must necessarily be many shipwrecks: every hint by which the distress of our fellow creatures may be alleviated, or any saving of property made to individuals in such situations, should be communicated for their good. As the Members of the Royal Society have it in their power to make such hints most universally known, I have been induced, from their readiness to receive every useful information, to lay before them a particular account of the success attending a method for the safe removal of ships that have been driven on shore, and damaged in their bottoms, to places, (however distant) for repairing them; I hope, therefore, they will excuse the liberty I have taken in presenting this to them. Should the Society honour me by recording it, it will make me the most ample satisfaction for my attention to it, and afford me the greatest pleasure.

On January the 1st, 1779, in a most dreadful storm, the *York* East Indiaman, of eight hundred tons, homeward bound, with a pepper cargo, parted her cables in Margate Roads, and was driven on shore, within one hundred feet of the head and thirty feet of the side, of Margate Pier, then drawing twenty-two feet six inches of water, the flow of a good spring tide being only fourteen feet at that place.

On the third of the same month I went down, as a shipbuilder, to assist as much as lay in my power my worthy friend Sir Richard Hotham, to whom the ship belonged. I found her perfectly up-right, and her shere (or side appearance) the same as when first built, but sunk to twelve feet water mark fore and aft in a bed of chalk mixed with a stiff blue clay, exactly the shape of her body below that draft of water; and from the rudder being torn from her as she struck coming on shore, and the violent agitation of the sea after her being there, her stern was so greatly injured as to admit free access thereto, which filled her for four days equal to the flow of the tide. Having fully informed my self of her situation and the flow of the spring tides, and being clearly of the opinion she might be again got off, I recommended as the first necessary step, the immediate discharge of her cargo; and in the progress of that business, I found the tide always flowed to the same height on the ship, and when the cargo was half discharged, and I knew the remaining part should not make her draw more than eighteen feet of water, and while I was observing the water of twenty-two feet six inches by the ships marks, she instantly lifted to seventeen feet eight inches, the water and air being before excluded by her pressure on the clay, and the atmosphere acting upon her upper part equal to six hundred tons, which is the weight of water displaced at the difference of those two draughts of water.

The moment the ship lifted, I discovered she had received more damage than was at first apprehended, her leaks being such as filled her from four to eighteen feet water in one hour and a half. As nothing effectual was to be expected from pumping, several scuttles or holes in the ships side were made, and valves fixed thereto, to draw off the water to the lowest ebb of the tide, to facilitate the discharge of the remaining part of the cargo; and, after many attempts, I succeeded in an external application of sheep skins sewed on a sail, and thrust under the bottom, to stop the body of water from rushing so furiously into the ship. This business affected, moderate pumping allowed us to keep the ship to about six feet water at low water, and by vigorous effort we could bring the ship so light as (when the cargo should be all discharged) to be easily removed into deeper water. But as the external application might be disturbed by so doing, or totally removed by the agitation of the ship, it was absolutely necessary to provide some permanent security for the lives of those who were to navigate her to the River Thames. I then recommended, as the cheapest, quickest, and most effectual plan, to lay a deck in the hold, as low as the water could be pumped to, framed so solidly and securely, and caulked so tight as to swim the ship independant of her own leaky bottom.

Beams of fir timber, twelve inches square, were placed in the hold under every lower deck beam in the ship, as low as water would permit; these were in two pieces, for the convenience of getting them down, and also for the better fixing them of an exact length, and well bolted together when in their place. Over these were laid long Dantzic deals of two inches and an half thick, well nailed and caulked. Against the ship's side, all fore and aft, was well nailed a piece of fir, twelve inches broad and six inches thick on the lower, and three inches on the upper edge, to prevent the deck from rising at the side. Over the deck, at every beam, was laid a cross piece of fir timber, six inches deep and twelve inches broad, reaching from the pillar of the hold to the ship's side, on which the shores were to be placed to resist the pressure of the water beneath. On each of these, and against the lower deck beam, at equal distance from the side and the middle of the ship, was placed an upright shore, six inches by twelve inches, the lower end let two inches into the cross piece. From the foot of this shore to the ship's side, under the end of every lower deck beam, was placed a diagonal shore, six inches by twelve, to ease the ship's deck of part of the strain by throwing it on the side. An upright shore, of three inches by twelve, was placed from the end of every cross piece to the lower deck beams at the side; and

The Deptford Green Yard. Leases taken by William Barnard 1780-87 from the Bridge House Estates

one of three inches by twelve on the midship end of every cross piece to the lower deck beam, and nailed to the pillars in the hold. Two firm tight bulkheads or partitions were made as near the extremes of the ship as possible. The ceiling or inside plank of the ship was securely caulked up to the lower deck, and the whole formed a complete ship with a flat bottom within side to swim the outside leaky one; and that bottom being depressed six inches below the external water, resisted the ship's weight above it, equal to five hundred and eight-one tons, and safely conveyed her to the dry dock at Deptford.

Since I wrote the above account I have been desired to use the same method on a Swedish ship stranded near Margate on the same day as the *York* East Indiaman, and swim her to London. [(104)]

Rental Book 1780-85.
Deptford Town and Strand.

'William Barnard assignee of Thomas West for the merchant yard and several tenements at £140 per annum.'
Rental Book 1786-7.

'William Barnard, assignee of Thomas West for a shipyard and several buildings late Titus West and several messuages adjoining late William Hales to him demised for 31 years from Christmas 1773 at £140 a year held to Christmas 1786. Lease then surrendered.'

'William Barnard, assignee of Joseph Hales for seven messuages or tenements part of another messuage, a stable, a piece of ground, and about 2 acres of garden ground on the south side of Anchorsmith Alley at Deptford to him demised for 21 years, from Lady Day 1777 at £20 a year - held to Christmas 1786. Lease then surrendered.'

'William Barnard for a shipwright's yard and several messuages or tenements and buildings at Deptford late Thomas West - and several messuages or tenements and two acres of garden ground and other premises at Deptford late Joseph Hales to him demised for 63 years from Christmas 1786 at £160 a year for the first two years at £300 a year for the residue of the term.'

William Barnard continues to appear in the Rentals Book of the Bridge House Estates until 1796 when the name of the tenant is changed to Frances Barnard executrix and sole legatee of William Barnard. The lease remained in her name until its expiry in the accountancy year 1849-50.

Appendix XII

"Success to Mr Barnard's Yard"
Inscription on a Chinese Export Porcelain Presentation Punch Bowl

In July 1988 the above bowl was bought by the National Maritime Museum, Greenwich (with financial help from the Friends of the Museum) from Spink & Son Ltd, who in turn had purchased it from Lawrence Fine Art of Crewkerne acting on behalf of a vendor who regrettably insisted upon anonymity.

Particulars as under

Period	Qianlong	circa 1785
Dimensions	Diameter	39.5cm.
	Height	17cm.

Description — Hand painted in grisaille with line drawings of ships in frame on the outer surface; the ships depicted are a hag-boat or merchant vessel of the mid 18c. and a frigate of the same period. Both vessels appear twice, the one alternating with the other and are set against a river background with strong oriental overtones. The rim is finely painted with a gold trellis border. The feet are decorated with a husk-chain pattern.

Inscription — The words "Success to Mr Barnard's Yard" are inscribed on the inner base surrounded by an Adamesque oval panel surmounted by medallions and ribbons.

Condition — Excellent apart from a small piece of unglaze on the feet. There has been no restoration.

Source of Drawings — The two vessels portrayed by the Chinese artist are copies of plates Nos.VIII and XXXVI which appear in Chapman's "Architectura Navalis Mercatoria" published in Stockholm in 1768, the former plate illustrates the bow and starboard side of an unrigged hag-boat and the latter the stern and aft section of the starboard side of a frigate in frame.

The bowl viewed from three different aspects, giving a complete picture of the bowl's outer decoration

Appendix XIII

Frances Barnard c.1736 - 1825

The eighty eight years and some nine months of the life of Frances Barnard bridged an era of unrest and upheaval. The Britain of the early and mid eighteenth century bore very little relation to the Britain of 1825. The successive wars of the period, the French Revolution, the expansion of the Empire to include India and Canada, the loss of the thirteen Colonies in North America, the rise and fall of Napoleon brought in their wake a rate of change in social conditions which may possibly be best exemplified by the contrast in male apparel which occurred during the period. Frances, living almost until the dawn of the age of Queen Victoria (born 1819) would have remembered when a man of fashion was resplendent in a tricorn hat, wore a tied-back powdered wig, a flowered silk waistcoat, a gold braided jacket with enormous cuffs and silver or gold buttons. Beneath he wore knee breeches with white stockings and his shoes were adorned with silver buckles. By the year 1825 the more practical but sombre coloured suit and trousers had become the fashion. Both reflected the age in which they flourished.

For a greater part of her life the elements, in the form of water and wind, were supreme in the fields of power and propulsion - as they had been for millenniums - but Frances would live to see the use of steam and the introduction of the paddle and screw to propel waterborne vessels. In her last years she experienced the beginning of the railway boom.

In common with a majority of women of her time the first decades of her marriage were given over to childbearing, her first child William being born in June 1764 - the year in which her husband began his shipbuilding career on the Thames - and from then on, at more or less regular intervals, she bore another seven children, the last, Elizabeth, being baptized in June 1780 - a year which coincided with her husband's purchase of the lease of the Deptford Green Yard. Frances, as was then commonplace, suffered the loss of a number of her children for in 1771 and 1772 she lost a child either at or shortly after birth. In 1773 she suffered a further and more devastating loss when her first child, William, died at only nine years of age. Fifteen years later, in 1795, she had to endure an even greater blow for in his fifty ninth year her husband died after a long illness. Frances was then some fifty seven years of age.

The death of William was a watershed in her life for from being a housewife and mother she was suddenly catapulted into the limelight as senior partner of the family business, a state of affairs brought about by a bequest in her husband's Will by which his estate passed to 'his beloved wife'. There can be little doubt that the thirty five years Frances spent at her husband's side gave her an insight into the shipbuilding business both in respect of the success which could be achieved and the pit-falls which could ensnare the unfortunate. In respect of the latter it must be recalled that in 1781 she had given a home to her father-in-law, John Barnard, when penniless and homeless after his bankruptcy. He died at her home in Deptford Green in 1774.

With Frances as senior partner the style of the firm became Frances Barnard & Co. It is extremely doubtful whether Frances played any role in the day-to-day running of the company but as its owner she controlled the purse-strings and as a result must have been party to all matters concerning finance, a matter of major concern to any merchant shipbuilding business. At the time of her husband's death the business was under the control of an able foreman who had been in her husband's service for some twenty five years. Her two sons William and Edward George were still serving their apprenticeships being nineteen and seventeen years of age respectively. Both became partners when qualified.

The elder son William proved to be a man cast in the mould of his forebears and during his years in charge of the daily running of the business the firm prospered. So satisfactory was his management that in 1803 Frances felt it safe to take partial retirement. She was some sixty seven years of age. With her two unmarried daughters she moved to Ravensbury Manor House, Mitcham, Surrey, a most desirable residence standing in twelve acres of parkland on the north bank of the River Wandel. She retained her position of senior partner. The peace of mind she hoped to enjoy in her new surroundings was short-lived for in 1805 her son William died. He was in his twenty ninth year. The younger son Edward George stepped into his brother's shoes only to find that the boom days in the shipbuilding industry were on the wane as the march of world events brought about a drastic fall in the demand for both naval vessels and merchantmen. Notwithstanding an ever deteriorating situation Frances battled on until her death in 1825. Her life had seen the wheel of fortune turn full circle, she had seen a small country business develop into a major player in the maritime affairs of the nation, she had then seen orders drop away and business fall into decay. Fortunately for her the state of her personal finances isolated her from any distress caused by the collapse of the shipping industry. She died a rich woman.

Her will shows that at Ravensbury she had surrounded herself with memorabilia of her shipbuilding career for in her will she bequeathed to Edward George:

"All pictures, models, draughts of ships drawings, instruments, moulds cabinets of woods and such printed books as are anyway related to the art of shipbuilding."

The Will also directed that a Trust Fund be set up for her children, the assets of which included freehold and leasehold properties, farms and lands.

Edward George, free of his mother's constraint, virtually abandoned shipbuilding in order to enjoy the life of a country gentleman.

Appendix XIV

The *Warren Hastings* and *La Piémontaise*

The *Warren Hastings* was among the largest East Indiamen of her day and was involved in one of the most famous sea-battles to be found in the chronicles of the H.E.I.C. Sailing from Portsmouth to China on her second voyage in February 1805, with Capt Thomas Larkins in command, she mounted forty four guns and had a complement of one hundred and ninety six men and boys. Her homeward voyage from Canton commenced on 31 March 1806 in company with three other East Indiamen, one of which was the Barnard built *Dorsetshire* the 'property' of Robert Williams. A combination of unfortunate circumstances resulted in the *Warren Hastings* being separated from her companions leaving her alone in a part of the Indian Ocean regularly patrolled by French men-of-war. Regrettably, Capt Larkins had been either obliged, or tempted, to sacrifice armament for cargo by caulking up a number of gun-ports on the main deck, and to make matters worse, forty Chinese members of the crew had elected to remain in Canton and eighteen of the best of her English crew had been impressed for service aboard a warship. Her armament, when she sailed from Canton, amounted to only thirty six guns and she carried a crew of one hundred and thirty eight men and boys.

On 21 June 1806 the *Warren Hastings* was intercepted by the French frigate *La Piémontaise,* a recently launched, powerful and exceptionally fast vessel manned by a crew of 385 with a broadside weight of shot of 553lbs; a figure which compared with 312lbs for the *Warren Hastings*. Despite the great disparity in both guns and man-power Capt Larkins, for a period of some three and a quarter hours, fought off continuous French attacks. Great havoc was caused to the undermanned and lightly armed East Indiaman but the fate of the day was eventually decided when, with the gun-room ablaze and the fore and main mast wrecked, the mizzen-mast fell forward effectively blocking-up every gun on the upper deck. At 16.50 hours Capt Larkins, with the consent of his officers struck his colours. The action had cost the *Warren Hastings* seven killed and thirteen wounded, whilst the *La Piémontaise* had suffered seven killed and five wounded.

Unhappily the accepted civilized behaviour of the victor towards the vanquished conventionally observed once a vessel had struck its colours was brutally ignored in this case by the shameful drunken behaviour of the 1st Lt Moreau, the officer commanding the boarding party sent aboard the *Warren Hastings* to take possession of her as a prize. Capt Larkins and other officers were seriously wounded and were extremely lucky to escape with their lives. Part of the official account of the incident as recorded by Capt Larkins, reads:

"This Moreau..... was most thoroughly incapacitated from either the performance of a generous disposition as a man, or of his duty as an officer or a seaman, for he was as furiously intoxicated as the lowest, vilest wretch, who followed and abetted him in his murderous and bloodthirsty intentions. His myrmidons, spread about the ship, were reviling and treating in the most shameful and inhuman manner all who could not escape from their fury, while this officer, having the whole of the upper deck to himself, was vaunting about with all the emptiness of self-sufficiency, and, in the paroxysms of inebriation, was driving his poignards (having one in each hand) into every inoffensive thing that happened to lay in his way, such as the capstan, the fallen mizzen-mast, the coamings of the after-hatchway etc., presuming as may very properly be concluded, that these objects of his indignation had not the power to return the insults, or, that the fumes of liquor had so very forcibly overcome his eyesight that he did not know what he was doing. However, I am sensibly led to the former conclusion, drawing the inference from his conduct towards me - a fallen, defenceless enemy."

The captors took the *Warren Hastings* to the island of Mauritius where she was made seaworthy and entered into service with the French navy. Luckily she had the good fortune to be retaken by the British who returned her to her role as merchantman trading on the coast of India. The following account of a momentary re-union between Capt Larkins and his old ship written by the acting quartermaster of the *Warren Hastings III* * in 1808 makes emotive reading:

"We at last reached Saugar in safety, before we arrived there our feelings were excited to a high pitch of sympathy by an interesting scene. Captain Larkins was standing on the poop close by where I stood with his glass at his eye examining the ships which were lying at anchor when he suddenly exclaimed, "I surely know that ship lying yonder; my eyes cannot deceive me, it's my old ship, the *Warren Hastings*." The pilot was requested to go within hail of her. All hands were upon deck; every eye fixed on the strange ship, and soldiers and sailors manned the rigging. The Captain got the large speaking trumpet and bellowed out "What ship ahoy?" answer, "The *Warren Hastings*, what ship are you?" answer, "The new *Warren Hastings*." Here the shouting of the crews of both ships was quite deafening. Our Captain could not say a syllable more, but was much affected as to shed a tear to the memory of his old ship, which he had manfully defended, but lost to some ship of war."

---

* *Warren Hastings III* was built by Perry, a Thames shipbuilder

The *Warren Hastings* and *La Piémontaise* at the commencement of the engagement on 21 June 1806

The *Warren Hastings* and *La Piémontaise* following the battle

Edward George Barnard, politician 1832 - 1851

Edward George entered Parliament in 1832 when he became one of the two MPs for the newly created Parliamentary Division of the Borough of Greenwich. He retained his seat until his death contesting and winning in the General Elections of 1835, 1841 and 1847. He was a Whig. An entry in 'Whose Who in British Members of Parliament' describes him as "a shipbuilder in favour of the ballot, triennial Parliaments and the repeal of taxes etc."

It is difficult to perceive what he accomplished in his nineteen years in the House. Being of an independent turn of mind he did not always support the party line and would at times cast his vote with the opposition. In 1835, for instance, he voted with the minority in favour of admitting women into the visitors gallery of the House and in the same year, voted once again with the minority, in favour of a motion to petition the King to pardon certain Dorset labourers and to direct their recall from deportation. It was also said of him that he adopted an indifferent attitude towards his constituents and was careful not to place himself in a position where he would be beholden to any person or persons - such as lobby groups - for fear of being asked at some future date to vote against his better judgement.

The manner in which he attended to the business of the House of Commons was conscientious in the extreme. An obituary notice in the Kentish and Surrey Mercury of 21 June 1851 stated that :

"....no man ever exhibited more untiring zeal - he was generally almost the first man in the House and almost the last to leave it - and we venture to assert that during the long period he was in Parliament he was at more divisions than any other member and if the hours of his attendance were counted up they would exceed the total which any other member could have undertaken....the duration of his life has no doubt been shortened by the exhausting effect of mid-night sittings."

Unfortunately this dedication did not bring him promotion and he remained a backbencher until the end. His independence of mind would not have endeared him to his superiors but it is doubtful whether he ever hankered after high office. The tread-mill of the daily round must have satisfied some inner craving for his political career brought him neither financial gain nor social advancement. A publicity blurb published at the time of the 1832 General Election said of him:

"He seeks not laurels from the great, he counts not smiles from the opulent, he rests his fate upon public and honest principles,
and upon that and that alone...."
It appears a fair assessment of his character.

Barnard for Ever!

Our ship, boy, has weathered the storm,
And cast anchor now safely in port;
I've named her "*The Gallant Reform*,"
Which took possession of RUSSELL's strong fort.

No doubt she'll prove leaky, and bad,
Induring so many hard gales ;
But there's plenty of stuff to be had,
To give her topsides, and new wales.

We'll fit her for sea, boys, again,
And caulk up her seams, strong and tight ;
And while in the dock she remains,
Let's drink, to our jolly Shipwright !

We'll wish him success in his job,
And furnish materials, pure ;—
We will, one and all, bear a bob,
To make his election secure.

When the Pilot shall board her again,
And safely conduct her to sea,
May our Captain prove true to his men,—
And old England shall ever be free !

Then, success to the Pilot, EARL GREY !
Who so nobly has weathered the storm ;
For BROUGHAM, and ALTHORP, hurrah !
GEORGE BARNARD, our KING, and REFORM ! ! !

AGNESS BROWN, PRINTER, HIGH STREET, DEPTFORD.

Barnard for Ever ! ! !
OR, A CHIP OF THE OLD BLOCK.

As Reform is the question, pray let me impart,
To the ears of my friends, and to each honest heart,—
It's now in your power, which I am sure you'll all own,
To choose those who are stanch, and sound to the back-bone.
Tol de rol.

There's many a Tory will now put on a Wig,
And disguised in false colours, he'll whistle a jig ;
If you dance to the figure, you'll surely get floored,
For the Ship's named *Deception*, which Britons wont board.
Tol de rol.

Now the wood she was built with, had got the dry-rot,
Which BARNARD found out,—be it never forgot,
He saved Captain and Crew from the merciless storm,
And is now made Commander of the good Ship *Reform*.
Tol de rol.

Success to the Captain, and his bold jolly crew !
When they touch British land, may their wives, ever true,
Join both heart and hand, sing out, Orange for ever,
NED BARNARD's the boy, from him we'll ne'er sever !
Tol de rol.

Now this is his maxim,—then doubt it, who can !
He's a guardian and shield to the hard-working man ;
May health, wealth, and honor, still add to his stock,—
When he cuts his cable, we'll have a Chip of the Block.

Agness Brown, Printer, High Street, Deptford.

Electioneering handbills

Free and Independent
ELECTORS
OF THE
BOROUGH
OF
Greenwich.

BROTHER ELECTORS,

The time is nearly arrived when the opportunity of our exercising that great and glorious prerogative of Englishmen—returning our own Members to Parliament—will be placed in our hands. REMEMBER! it was the Reform Bill, that triumph of Reason over Despotism, which gave us this privilege; consequently, it is that Bill, in effect, which our Country NOW CALLS UPON US strenuously to support.

The Bill of itself (unless its ulterior beneficial objects be carried,) is a mere non-entity. To maintain, therefore, this all-important principle, becomes our chief object. It behoves us to uphold, with all the power we possess, the views and interest of that party, who, possessed of every domestic comfort and happiness, is ready and willing to sacrifice all for his Country's cause. BROTHER ELECTORS! shall it ever be said by posterity, that our hearts felt cool upon such a subject—a subject of such vital importance? No; never—never (I feel persuaded you will respond,) shall that charge be brought against us. I know your feelings well.—they are in perfect unison with my own. Be up then—stirring—rouse ye from your slumber, and support with vigour, courage, firmness, and determination, THE MAN BEST CALCULATED to carry those feelings into effect. Need I, Brother Electors, need I name that Man? Although well, and deservedly well, known amongst you,—I will; for the more often I hear that name repeated, the better it sounds, and the more I feel convinced that none other in the field is like him. BARNARD, then is the Man! the unflinching Friend of Reform,—the firm supporter of Truth and Justice,—the Enemy of Slavery and Oppression,—and the decided Friend of civil and religious Liberty. He seeks not LAURELS from the GREAT,—he courts not SMILES from the OPULENT,—he rests his fate upon public and honest principles, and upon that, and that alone, his claim is just, upon your suffrages. These qualifications, Brother Electors, are indisputable; as such, I need not intreat you to buckle on your armour;—enter the lists like Men,—fight, like Britons, the fair fight,—and victory must inevitably crown your great and glorious efforts.

An ELECTOR
OF THE BOROUGH OF GREENWICH.

8th December, 1832.

AGNESS BROWN, PRINTER, HIGH STREET, DEPTFORD

Electioneering poster praising the third Reform Bill of 7 June 1832

Appendix XVI

Gosfield Hall

The Manor of Gosfield has Saxon origins and following the Norman Conquest it was held by the nobleman Robert le Claire, Earl of Gloucester. In the following four centuries the estate passed through the hands of some six families - often through the female line.

The present hall originated in a defensible house built by Sir Thomas Wentworth between the years 1545-1560, it was constructed round a courtyard and was capable of resisting attack having no outside windows on the ground floor and only one fortified entrance set in the centre of the west wing. It is said to be the only Tudor mansion in England which has retained its original ground-plan although only the west wing has been preserved in its typical Tudor red-brick form. Internally, on the first floor, is the oak-panelled Queen's Room which extends the whole length of the building. Diamond-shaped leaded-windows overlook the quadrangle. The other three elevations of the original house have been rebuilt at different times by successive owners to meet their own personal requirements and in the style of the day. The Hall is said to have contained one hundred rooms and as many windows as there are days in a year.

The names given to certain rooms reflect both the history of the house as well as commemorating a number of owners, there is the King's Room; the Queen's Room, not to be confused with the Queen's Gallery; the Wentworth, and Nugent Rooms; the Prophet's, and Priest's Room together with the Old Drawing Room and Lattice Chamber.

The East Wing was fundamentally altered in the late seventeenth century when Sir Thomas Millington converted the original Tudor wing into a Grand Salon for use as a state banqueting hall.

The North Wing was reconstructed in the early eighteenth century by John Knight which among other improvements greatly enhanced the facilities of the Kitchen quarters. Later a magnificent Ballroom was built on the first floor by Roger Nugent the third husband of the widow of the above mentioned John Knight.

The rooms along the South front overlooking the lake and park were also the product of the Nugent era and included the Queens, Wentworth, Nugent and Prophet's rooms together with the family dining room, study and library.

Queen Elizabeth I was an early royal visitor to the Hall paying her first visit in the year 1561, only a year after the building was completed, she made another visit in 1579. On the first occasion she stayed for three nights and on the second for five. On a less harmonious note Lady Catherine Grey, the sister of Lady Jane Grey, was held in custody by Sir John Wentworth in the years 1566-7. Some two centuries later in 1748 Hugh Walpole, following a visit to the Hall, wrote that the house was 'extremely in fashion but did not answer me, though there are some fine things about it. The house is vast, built around a very old court which has never been fine and the old gallery, which is a bad narrow room. The rest of the house is all modernised and in patches and in bad taste...'

Robert Nugent, although a friend of the Prince of Wales, was considered by many to be a 'nouveau riche' upstart. In 1807 the Hall became a royal residence when the exiled, Louis XVIII, King of France, accepted the offer by the Marquis of Buckingham to make the Hall his temporary home in this country. He stayed, with his wife and court, for two years before moving to Hartwell House in Buckinghamshire.

The estate passed to the Buckingham family via the daughter of John Nugent by his third wife who had married George Temple, later to become Marquis of Buckingham. On his death in 1813 his son leased the Hall to Col Thomas Astle and following the death of this tenant the Hall was sold to Edward George Barnard in 1825.

Sources:
History and Description of Gosfield Hall, Essex. Pub. Wayfarers Trust Ltd (1956)
Restoration of an Elizabethan Mansion. Journal: The Illustrated Carpenter and Builder (Aug. 1956)
Gosfield Hall. Typescript History by Dr Guy Bar (Essex Record Office) (1966)
Gosfield Hall. General Account. Typescript history, signed AGT (Gosfield Hall Archives)
Gosfield Hall Estate Chronology. Unsigned typescript chronology from William I to Elizabeth II 1955. Has 58 dated entries (Gosfield Hall Archives)

Appendix XVII

Alphabetical ship-list of vessels built in Barnard Shipyards for the Navy Board, 1740-1813

Name	Rate	Guns	Launched	Name	Rate	Guns	Launched
Achilles	4	60	16.4.1757	Kite	sl.	10	17.7.1795
Adder	gb	12	22.4.1797	Litchfield	4	50	26.6.1746
Africa	3	64	14.4.1781	Locust	gb	12	2.4.1801
Alarm	5	32	19.9.1758	Majestic	3	74	11.2.1785
Ambuscade	5	32	17.9.1773	Mallard	gb	12	11.4.1801
Andromache	5	32	17.11.1781	Marlborough	3	74	22.6.1807
Arrogant	3	74	22.1.1761	Mercury	6	20	2.3.1756
Biddeford	6	20	15.6.1740	Northumberland	3	74	2.2.1798
Carnatic	3	74	21.1.1783	Orion	3	74	1.6.1787
Centurion	4	50	27.5.1774	Orpheus	5	32	7.5.1774
Champion	6	24	17.5.1779	Orpheus	5	32	3.6.1780
Charon	5	44	8.10.1778	Pactolus	5	38	14.8.1813
Colchester	4	50	14.8.1744	Pandora	6	24	17.5.1779
Conquerer	3	70	24.5.1758	Parthian	sl	10	13.2.1808
Contest	gb	12	11.4.1797	Pelican	6	24	24.4.1777
Cormorant	sl	14	21.5.1776	Proserpine	6	28	7.7.1777
Cornwall	3	74	16.1.1812	Quebec	5	32	14.7.1760
Crash	gb	12	5.4.1797	Repulse	3	74	21.7.1803
Devonshire	3	74	23.9.1812	Robust	3	74	25.10.1764
Diamond	5	38	17.3.1794	Rodney	3	74	8.12.1809
Druid	sl	10	21.3.1761	Savage	sl	14	28.4.1778
Dryad	5	36	4.6.1795	Scipio	3	64	22.10.1782
Eagle	4	58	2.12.1745	Seahorse	6	24	13.9.1748
Elk	sl	18	22.8.1804	Severn	4	50	10.7.1747
Eolus	5	32	28.2.1801	Solebay	5	36	26.3.1785
Experiment	4	50	23.8.1774	Spanker	fl.bat.		14.6.1794
Falcon	sl	10	12.11.1744	Spiteful	gb	12	24.4.1797
Granado	bm		22.6.1742	Sultan	3	74	23.12.1775
Hampshire	4	50	13.11.1741	Sylph	sl	18	8.9.1795
Harrier	sl	18	22.8.1804	Terrible	3	74	4.9.1762
Harwich	4	50	22.12.1742	Terror	bm		16.1.1759
Hector	3	74	27.5.1774	Tortoise	lighter		17.7.1780
Hound	sl	14	8.3.1776	Tremendous	3	74	30.10.1784
Hydra	6	24	8.8.1778	Triton	5	32	5.9.1796
Inconstant	5	36	28.10.1783	Vestal	5	32	17.6.1757
Inflexible	3	64	7.3.1780	York	3	64	24.3.1796
Iris	5	32	2.5.1783	Zealous	3	74	25.6.1785
Irresistible	3	74	6.12.1782	Zebra	sl	14	8.4.1777
				Zephyr	sl	14	31.5.1779

gb = gun boat, sl = sloop, bm = bomb ship, fl.bat. = floating battery

Analysis of rates and other types of vessels built in Barnard Yards for the Navy Board 1740 - 1813

3rd	4th	5th	6th	Sloop	Gun
22	10	15	8	12	6

Bomb Ship	Floating Battery	Store lighter
2	1	1

Alphabetical ship-list of vessels built for the shipping interests of the Hon East India Company in Barnard Shipyards 1763-1825.

Name	Tons	Husband	Voyages	Service
Ankerwick	679	Barrington Buggin	4	1764-74
Airley Castle	813	Robert Williams	8	1787-1806
Arniston	1433	John Wedderbourn	8	1790-1812
Asia III	958	Henry Bonham	10	1811-31
Brilliant	703	Sir William James	1	1781
Bridgewater I	804	John Wood	4	1769-79
Bridgewater II	799	Nicholas Skottowe	6	1785-97
Baring	820	Robert Charnock	6	1801-12
Boddam	1021	George Palmer	6	1787-1800
Clinton	711	William Larkins	?	1786-??
Caledonian	612	Robert Charnock	2	1797-1800
Dutton	761	Capt Henry Rice	5	1781-93
Dunira	1325	Geo. Palmer	8	1817-31
Dorsetshire	1260	Robert Williams	9	1800-21
Earl Fitzwilliam	803	James Farquharson	5	1786-96
Enfield	1021	?	?	1787
Earl St Vincent	818	John Pascall Larkins	7	1799-1811
Fairford	755	Geo. Ramsey	1	1781
General Barker	758	John Durand	1	1778
General Coate	787	Robert Williams	6	1781-94
Granby	786	Chas. Raymond	4	1767-78
Hinchinbrooke	528	Robert Williams	1	1780
Hindustan I	1248	Robert Williams	2	1789-1793
Hindustan II	1463	Robert Williams	4	1796-1803
Hythe	1333	Stewart Majorbanks	6	1820-30
Lord Nelson	818	Robert Charnock	5	1799-1807
Lord Lowther	1332	Henry Blanchard	4	1825-30
Mars	696	Capt Wm. Farrington	1	1785
Marquis of Lansdown	647	Antony Brough	5	1786-98
Marquis of Wellington	961	Henry Bonham	9	1812-28
Melville Castle	806	David Webster	7	1786-99
Metcalf	819	James Thomas	6	1804-14
Middlesex	755	Robert Williams	5	1783-93
Mount Stuart	758	Geo. Ramsey	2	1777-79

Nepture II	758	Andrew Moffat	4	1780-7
Ponsbourne I	499	Thos. Lane	4	1765-72
Ponsbourne II	758	Thos. Lane	6	1780-93
Phoenix	818	Robert Williams	6	1804-17
Preston	671	Wm. Hamilton	6	1798-1809
Prince Regent	953	Henry Bonham	10	1811-32
Prince William Henry	803	James Farquharson	5	1787-1800
Princess Amelia I	808	Robert Williams	4	1786-96
Princess Amelia II	1275	Robert Williams	10	1808-25
Resolution	804	Mark Cramer	4	1769-78
Rockingham	798	Sir Richard Hotham	7	1785-99
Royal Admiral	914	Sir Richard Hotham	8	1777-95
Royal Bishop	720	Robert Williams	2	1777-86
Royal Charlotte II	855	Albert Nesbit	5	1771-85
Royal Henry	499	Thomas Lane	4	1771-81
Sir William Pultney	565	John Locke	6	1805-14
Speaker	499	Andrew Moffatt	4	1763-71
Sulivan	755	Robert Williams	6	1782-96
Taunton Castle	1198	Peter Esdaile	9	1790-1810
Thames II	1330	Abel Chapman	7	1819-32
Thomas Coutts	1334	Sir Robert Preston	8	1817-31
Varunna	526	John Prinsep	4	1796-1803
Warren Hastings I	716	William Larkins	6	1781-94
Warren Hastings II	1200	John Pascall Larkins	2	1802-6
Walmer Castle	1200	John Pascall Larkins	9	1796-1814
William Pitt	819	Henry Bonham	7	1805-19
Windsor	1332	Felix Clay	7	1818-31
Winterton	771	Thos. Newte	4	1782-91

In addition to the above named East Indiamen the following small vessels were built in the Barnard yards:-

Antelope, a packet of	276 tons	1781
Bentley, a hoy of	129 tons	1802
Blucher, a hoy of	69 tons	1815
Madras, a hoy of	86 tons	1786

Analysis of owners

An analysis of the list shows that the Barnard family built 62 East Indiamen for 36 different owners and that 10 owners contracted for more than one vessel apiece. The Robert Williams, father and son, topped the list with orders for 11 vessels.

Other multiple owners:-

The Larkins family	5 vessels
Henry Bonham	4 "
Thomas Lane	3 "
Robert Charnock	3 "
Andrew Moffatt	2 "
Sir Richard Hotham	2 "
James Farquharson	2 "
Geo. Ramsey	2 "

Appendix XVIII

The Wreck of the East Indiaman *Winterton*

The East Indiaman *Winterton*, a vessel of some 876 tons, was launched from the Grove St Yard, Deptford in the year 1782. She was wrecked on the coast of Madagascar on the evening of Sunday 20 August 1792.

The ill fated voyage, destined for Madras and Bengal, commenced on 2 May 1792. Captained by George Dundas her passengers and crew numbered between 270 and 280 persons. The weather was kindly. The island of Madeira was passed and no other land was seen until the vessel rounded the Cape of Good Hope on 18 July. A short stop-over at False Bay and on 10 August the *Winterton* departed for India. Capt Dundas decided to bear up the inner or Mozambique Channel but unfortunately light and contrary winds made it impossible for him to reach St Augustine's Bay on the island of Madagascar. Nevertheless lunar observations made on 16–17 August reasonably assured him that he was on the right course. Sunday 19 August brought favourable winds, Capt Dundas was nevertheless unusually concerned, for although he was aware land was near, he had no knowledge of its exact distance; information essential for night navigation. On the evening of Sunday 19 August Capt Dundas retired to his cabin at about 22.00 hours but was again on deck at midnight when he made a number of alterations to the vessel's course. In addition crewmen were stationed on the bowsprit and foreyard. A little before 0.300 hours Capt Dundas gave it as his opinion that the vessel was some 60 miles from land. Some seven or eight minutes later the vessel struck; she had gone aground on an uncharted reef. The water was as smooth as a mill pond; no breakers were visible. Every soul that could move was speedily on deck. All efforts were made to free the vessel but to no avail. The fact that she had grounded at night at the top of the spring tides greatly diminished the chances of successfully refloating her. The vessel was stranded on a reef some six miles from land in the region of point St Felix. Daylight, the ebbing tide and the threatened break up of the vessel's bottom timbers showed the Captain and his officers just how perilous the situation had become. The safety of the passengers thereby became paramount. A yawl, under the command of the second mate and purser, was sent ashore to ascertain the safest possible landing place. On Monday evening Capt Dundas called the people together and in a short speech advised them on the route they should take when safely ashore. All hope of saving the ship had been abandoned. The boats to be used to ferry the passengers ashore were moored a considerable way astern. The strong running surf continued to beat against the wreck with furious violence and disastrous consequences – at midnight the boats moored astern were overset. The piercing shouts of the drowning men mingling with the loud roaring of the surf, the darkness of the night and the violence of the wind prevented any effectual means of aid. The chances against rescue of the ten endangered men seemed innumerable yet three were miraculously preserved. On the other hand the boats which had been the mens main prop were gone and the violence of the wind and surf made it doubtful whether the wreck would hold together till morning.

As dawn broke on 21 August the only remaining grounds for hope were centred on the making of rafts, anything that could float was pressed into service. It was observed that whatever went overboard drifted in-shore – a hopeful sign. Three or four rafts to carry 60 people were speedily assembled, and, although stopped for a time by the inner reef, they got safely ashore when the tide flowed. No further attempts were made to land that day. Whilst the above proceedings were in course the poop of the *Winterton* was being converted into another raft.

It was the carpenter, an active intelligent man, who had suggested that the poop could be converted into a raft by cutting scuttles at proper distances through the deck and lashing six empty butts upon it for buoyancy. His suggestion was carried out under Mr Dale's active superintendancy. However it could not be launched that day due to the state of the tide and to attempt to land it at night was thought too hazardous, however, circumstances conspired that a night landing became imperative. In fact, as the ship began to break up the poop began to separate from the wreck whereupon the lashings which held it to the stricken vessel were promptly cut and the poop floated free with some 80 to 100 people aboard. With the assistance of boards which were used as paddles, the survivors made their way through the surf to the shore. About the same number of people remained aboard without any support. Huge waves continued to pound the vessel and one of more than common fury sent a portion of the starboard side crashing into the raging sea. Many passengers were washed overboard and drowned. A few, once again in a miraculous fashion survived. Two young ladies going out to friends in India and a young girl of 12 years of age, were amongst those lost.

All forenoon the ladies had been standing on deck under the lee of the starboard side. Towards four o'clock in the afternoon they were conducted to the cabin of the Chief Mate, a haven which proved to be only temporary as rain, sea water and wind ultimately penetrated their sanctuary and they returned to the roundhouse which, wet and dreary as it was, was a little more raised above the surf. Tragically this too was carried away when the starboard section of the ship was lost.

The wreck had long been heeling to the starboard side whilst her stern was kept towards the surf by means of a hawser and anchor which had been laid earlier: but the fury of the surf could not be withstood for any great length of time.

Eventually, between 6 and 7 o'clock in the evening, the hawser snapped and the ship hove round with her broadside to the rocks where she was relentlessly pounded by the frenzied seas. Capt Dundas bravely remained on his ship until its last moment and was then taken aboard a raft. Regrettably the raft was overcrowded and a mighty wave washed him overboard; he disappeared into the night and the billowing surf. The number lost at this time was in the region of 48. One raft holding 50 to 60 persons drifted for a considerable time towards the shore grounding on a reef at about 11 o'clock at night. It floated off again on the flood tide at about 3 o'clock in the morning. After various adventures, which is not part of this narrative, the members of that party safely reached their different destinations.

There are no recorded accounts of the *Winterton*'s last days but it is fair to assume that, in the condition to which she had been reduced and the situation in which she lay, it can only have been a relatively short period of time before she was reduced to driftwood. A sad end to a proud product of man's enduring ingenuity.

Notes and references

1. Thos Fuller, History of Worthies of England 1662 BL LB31c 6660, Vol 1 p59
2. Journal of Sir Thomas Thornhill 1711
3. Tacket St collection: Church Book. "An account of the persons admitted into the church formerly under the pastoral care of Mr John Langston, now of Mr Benjamin Glanfield, also of the transactions relating to the church" 1686-1791 Suffolk Record Office (Ipswich) FK 3/1/115
4. Ipswich Guild of Freemen. The Great Court Books SROC5/14/7
5. Extracts from the Ipswich Corporation Records made by V.B. Redstone
   SRO (Ips.) ECR VolXXII No 48
6. Land Tax assessments for Wix Bishop 1702-10: Poor Rate for Wix Bishop 1711:Poor Rate St Clements 1718-66: Churchwardens Rate for St Clements 1727-81 SRO (Ips.) K30/2/2
7. Thomason Bloomfield and Mary Hubbard, exors. of a Mr. Hubbard. Land Tax assessments 1702-1711 SRO (Ips.) K 30/2/2
8. John Barnard's apprenticeship to Edmund Gooday. The Great Court Books SRO (Ips.) C/5/14/8
9. Indenture 30.11.1728 between Arthur Barnardiston and Edmund Gooday. SRO (Ips.) HD 6: 1/1
10. John Barnard the Younger. On his death the Ipswich Journal of 9.10.1784 reported that he was in his 80th year
11. Dissenters' Chapel, Tacket St "300 Years of Witness" Pub. 1980 by Christ Church, Tacket St, Ipswich.
12. Churchwarden's Rate Book, 1734 onward. SRO (Ips.) K 30/2/2
13. Admiralty Orders 4th and 8th October 1739 Public Record Office ADM 95/12
14. Complaints re caulking PRO ADM 2/472
15. *Biddeford* safely transported to Harwich PRO ADM 106/926
16. Admiralty order 28th April 1740 PRO ADM 95/12
17. John Barnard's letter to Navy Board re John's Ness PRO ADM 106/916
18. Protection of shipwrights PRO ADM 106/913
19. Protection of shipwrights Ibid
20. Supply of timber PRO ADM 106/913
21. Request for anchors and cables for *Hampshire* Ibid
22. *Granado* Bombship Ibid
23. Proposed return of the King's Yard to full establishment PRO ADM 106/2554
24. Survey of King's Yard, Harwich Ibid
25. Barnard proposes to rent the King's Yard PRO ADM 106/2557
26. Loss of the *Colchester* PRO ADM 106/1005
27. " " Court's Martial PRO ADM 1/5284
28. " " Master's Log PRO ADM 52/561
29. Wreck of the *Colchester* PRO ADM 106/1005
30. Stores for the *Centurion* Ibid
31. " " Ibid
32. " " Ibid
33. The Royal Yacht, *Caroline* Ibid
34. French privateers Ibid
35. Launch of the *Litchfield* PRO ADM 106/1023
36. " " Ibid
37. " " Ibid
38. " " Ibid
39. Defence of the King's Yard, Harwich PRO ADM 106/1005
40. The *Seahorse* and the Harwich Mail Packet PRO ADM 106/1054
41. Request to rent King's Yard, Harwich Ibid
42. Payment for timber PRO ADM 106/1079
43. Repair of fencing at the King's Yard PRO ADM 106/1088
44. Purchase of Nova Scotia Shipyard SRO (Ips.) EL 1/3/3
45. Contract for the *Conqueror* PRO ADM 95/12
46. Parliamentary Committee. British Library BS ref. 19, Reports and Papers
47. Launch of the *Conquerer*. Death of launch master. Ipswich Journal 24.5.1758
48. Court's Martial. Loss of *Conquerer* PRO ADM 1/5299
49. Launch of the *Achilles* PRO ADM 106/1118
50. " *Robust* PRO ADM 106/1132
51. Princess Charlotte of Mecklenburg. East Anglian Misc. Part I. Jan. 1940
52. Extracts from the letter from Rev. William Gordon to his god-daughter, Mrs M.J. Conder, concerning the building of the *Speaker*. Letter dated 2.1.1763. SRO (Ips.) FK 3/1/6/16
53. Misc. "In Letters" period 1771-80 PRO ADM 106/1194: 1207: 1223: 1226 1233:1242: 1246: 1255

54. Argyle breakwater danger to launch of *Centurion* PRO ADM 106/1223

55. Renewal of lease of King's Yard PRO ADM 106/1226

56. East Country oak. Breach of contract Ibid

57. John Turner Jnr. *Cormorant* to be built at Nova Scotia Ibid

58. Bankruptcy. Letter from Navy Board to Admiralty. PRO ADM 106/2208

59. London Gazette 27th February - 3rd March 1781

60. Daniel Defoe, Character of the late Dr S. Annesley (1697)

61. Chapter VIII Honourable East India Company. Refs. "Lords of the East" by Jean Sutton: "East Indiamen" by Sir Evan Cotton edited by Sir Chas. Fawcett: "Life of Clive" by G.W. Forrest

62. Grove St East Indiamen. 1763-82. Brit. Lib. India Office. Ship List of Master Attendant's Office. L/MAR/C 529

63. Request to undock *Levant* for East Indiaman PRO ADM 106/1197

64. Royal Yards and Merchant Builders compete for shipwrights on the Thames. PRO ADM 106/117

65. Financial affairs and arrangements between Adams and his partners extracted from evidence to the Court of Chancery 1792-93 Ref. 62

66. Misc. "In Letters" period 23rd Feb. 1776 - 7th July 1779. PRO ADM 106/1233

67. Improper impressment of Joseph Dyer Ibid

68. "History of Deptford" Nathanial Dews 1884: "enormous profits on capital induced the company (H.E.I.C.) to purchase land adjacent to the Royal Dockyard, and near the mouth of the Ravensbourne, where these adventurers formed a dockyard, storehouses etc. (...) the company (...) abandoned their shipbuilding enterprise after a destructive fire" p.270

69. Delayed launch of the *Tremendous* and *Majestic*. PRO ADM 106/1281

70. Misc. "In Letters" 1781-3 PRO ADM 106/1263

71. William Barnard's last letter to the Navy Board. PRO ADM 106/1454

72. William Barnard Jnr. request permission to launch floating battery PRO ADM 106/1454

73. William Barnard Snr. gives notice to wreck partnership PRO C12/4245

74. Court of Chancery PRO C/12/1401/4: C/12/2424/5

75. William Barnard reports death of his father PRO ADM 106/1454

76. Conversion of East Indiaman to naval vessel Ibid

77. " " " Ibid

78. " " " Ibid

79. Contract for the East Indiaman *Preston*. National Maritime Museum SCS/1 Shipbuilding 2. MS 8072

80. Tonnage of East Indiamen British Library Master Attendant Office L/Mar/C529

81. Request from Thames shipbuilders for financial relief PRO ADM 106/1456

82. Reply to foregoing addressed to Perry, Wells, Green Ibid

83. Memo. re whereabouts of Navy Board letter of 20 Jan 1801 Ibid

84. Request for protection from striking caulkers and sawyers Ibid

85. Endorsement to Navy Board letter of 28 July 1802 Ibid

86. Confirmation of protection by Sec. of State Ibid

87. John Dudman reports attack by strikers Ibid

88. Frances Barnard and Co. thank Navy Board for assistance during strike Ibid

89. Will of William Barnard (II), probate 11. 1420 PRO

90. Misc. "In Letters" period 1805-1813 PRO ADM 106/1457,8,9

91. Request for permission to launch *Pactolus* PRO ADM 106/1460

92. Acquisition of Rotherhithe Yard BL L/MAR/C/27(2)

93. Letter to Chancellor of the Exchequer dated 18 January 1814 from a consortium of Thames shipbuilding companies requesting protection from proposed India Shipping Bill. BL Volume for Assessions 1783-1835 Liverpool papers Vol CCXXI(ff467)1802-18

94. Letter to the Rt. Hon Lord Liverpool dated 30 June 1814, personally signed by partners of the companies referred to in (93) above and again requesting protection Ibid

95. Minutes of the Worshipful Committee for the Improving Navigation on the River Thames. Corporation of London. Port of London Auth. Records

96. Other minutes as above

97. Letter from E.G. Barnard II to the Prime Minister, Mr Gladstone dated 4 June 1873 BL Vol. of Assessions 1783-1835 Gladstone Papers Vol CCCLIV (ff330) June-August 1873

98. Apprenticeship Indenture of Henry Barnard 1591 Norfolk and Harwich Genealogical Soc. Vol XI (1979) p.21 "Gt. Yarmouth Apprenticeship Indentures 1563/1665" by Paul Rutledge

99. Will of John Barnard the Elder SRO 1C/AA1/145/78

100. "Recollections of a Deacon" SRO FK/3/1/11/7

101. Letter of Rev D. Edwards to Dr Conder SRO FK/3/1/11/1

102. Bank statements of John Barnard the Younger Barclay's Bank Plc.

Archives and Records, Wythenshore, Manchester

103. Admiralty instructions to the commander of the *Pandora* PRO ADM 2/120

104. William Barnard's paper to The Royal Society 1779 Royal Society Philosophical Transactions Annual Register 1780. Vol 3

Bibliography

A passenger on the ship	*A Narrative of the Loss of the* Winterton *East Indiaman*. Edinburgh (1820)
Abell, Sir Westcott	*The Shipwrights Trade*. Cambridge Press, Cambridge. (1948)
Arnott, W.G.	*The Orwell Estuary*. Boydell Press, Ipswich. (1954)
Banbury, Philip	*Shipbuilders of the Thames & Medway*. David & Charles, Newton Abbot. (1971)
Blankley, T.R.	*A Naval Compositor*. Reprint of 1750 publication by E. Owen, London. (1988)
Boudroit, Jean	*The Seventy four gun ship Vols 1-4*. Translated from the French by D.H. Roberts. Pub. Jean Boudroit Rotherfield, East Sussex. (1986)
British Library, India Office	Master Attendants Records Ref L/MAR/C/529
British Library, H.C. Hardy	*Register of ships, 1760-1812*
Chapman, Fredrick	*Architectura Navalis Mercatoria*. Facsimile of English translation by Adlard Coles. (1813) (1971)
Colledge, J.J.	*Ships of the Royal Navy Vol 1*. David & Charles, Newton Abbot. (1969)
Cotton, Sir Evan	*East Indiamen*. The Batchworth Press, London. (1949)
Deane, Sir Anthony	*Doctrine of Naval Architecture 1670*. Conway Press. Introductionand subscription notes by Brian Lavery. (1981)
Dews, N.	*History of Deptford*. Simkin & Marshall, London. (1884)
Dodd, James & Moore, J.	*Building the Wooden Fighting Ship*. Hutchinson, London. (1984)
Fincham, John	*A History of Naval Architecture*. Whittaker & Co., London 1851, reprinted by Scolar Press, London (1979).
Goodwin, Peter	*HMS Granado*. Conway Maritime Press, London. (1989)
	Sailing Men of War 1650-1850. Conway Maritime Press, London. (1987)
Greenhill, Basil and Manning, Sam	*Evolution of the Wooden Ship*. B.T. Batsford, London. (1988)
Holland, A.J.	*Buckler's Hard*. Kenneth Mason, Emsworth, Hants. (1985)
	Ships of British Oak. David and Charles, Devon. (1971)
Howard, Dr Frank	*Sailing Ships of War 1400-1860*. Conway Maritime Press, London. (1979)
Jones, A.G.E.	*Shipbuilding in Ipswich 1700-50*. Mariners Mirror, Vol 43 Nov. 1957
	Shipbuilding in Ipswich 1750-1800. Mariners Mirror, Vol 58 May 1972
Lavery, Brian	*The Ship of the Line, Vol 1 & 2*. (1984)
	The Line of Battle. (1992)
	Building the Wooden Walls. (1991)
	All published by Conway Maritime Press, London.
Lyon, David	*The Sailing Navy List*. Conway Maritime Press, London. (1993)
Malster, Robert	*Ipswich, Town on the Orwell*. Terence Dalton, Lavenham, Suffolk. (1978)
McKay, John and Coleman, R.	*HMS Pandora 1779*. Conway Maritime Press, London. (1992)
Ollivier, Blaise	*Eighteenth century Shipbuilding*. Reprinted with notes from 1737 original. Jean Boudroit Publication, Rotherfield, East Sussex. (1992)
Pool, Bernard	*Navy Board Contracts 1660-1832*. William Clowes. London & Beccles. (1966)
Pope, Dudley	*England Expects*. Weidenfeld & Nicolson, London. (1959)
Redstone, Lilian J.	*Ipswich through the Ages*. East Anglia Magazine, Ipswich. (1948)
Rodger, N.A.M.	*The Wooden World*. William Collins, Glasgow. (1986)
Sutton, Jean	*Lords of the East*. Conway Maritime Press. London. (1981)
Warner, Oliver	*The Battle of the Nile*. B. T. Batsford, London. (1960)

Picture Credits

Thanks are due to the following:

Bodleian Library, University of Oxford p 28 top left; Christ Church Tacket St, Ipswich p 85 bottom left; Essex County Council Archives p 76 above and below; Ipswich Borough Council Museums and Galleries p 9, 10 above, 12 and 13, 24; London Borough of Lewisham p 4; Museum in Docklands PLA Collection p 75; Parham Park Ltd p 53 bottom right; Queensland Museum Australia p 89 all three pictures; Sotheby's p 38 and book jacket; Suffolk County Council Libraries and Heritage p 11, 28 top left, 83, 85 top right; The British Museum p 41, 42, 43 top left and right; The Corporation of London Records Office p 52; National Maritime Museum, Greenwich p 22, 25, 26, 27, 32, 34, 49, 50 above and below, 53 top left, 54, 56, 57 both top right, 57 bottom, 60, 61, 62, 65 top and bottom right, 67 top and bottom, 71, 74, 92 all three pictures, 95 above and below, end papers.

Index

A

Achilles 23, 24, 25, 99
Ackworth, Sir Jacob 15
Adament 53
Adams, Henry 2, 29, 38, 39, 40, 45, 46, 47, 50, 58, 59, 60, 70
Adder 63, 99
Africa 37, 51, 55, 99
Airley Castle 56, 100
Aix-la-Chapelle, Peace of 22
   " , Treaty of 22, 23, 41
Alarm 23, 24, 25, 99
Alexander's Bank 35, 36
Ambuscade 47, 49, 55, 99
Amiens, Treaty of 64
Andromache 51, 55, 99
Ankerwick 46, 100
Anne Jane 19
Antelope 56, 101
Argyle 30
Arniston 56, 100
Arrogant 23, 24, 99
Asia 71, 72, 100
Austrian Succession, War of 13, 17, 22, 41

B

Bagnold, G 20
Baring 66, 100
Barnardiston, Arthur 10
Barrier Reef 47, 88
Bayonnaise 49
Beaulieu 29, 38, 39, 45, 46, 47, 58
Bellerophon 65
Benger, John 19
Bently 66, 101
Best in Christendom 37
Biddeford 11, 12, 14, 15, 16, 99
Binmer, Mr 31
Bligh, Lt William 88
Blucher 72, 101
Board of the Admiralty 7
Boddam 56, 100
Bonham, Henry 66, 72, 100, 101

Bounty 47, 88
Bridge House Estates 45, 50, 61, 73, 91
Bridgewater 46, 56, 100
Brilliant 56, 100
Brough, Antony 100
Buck brothers 9
Buckler's Hard 39, 45, 50, 60, 70
Buggin, Barrington 46, 100
Burns, Robert 20

C

Caledonian 66, 100
Carnatic 51, 99
Caroline 26
Centurion 19, 30, 99
Champion 33, 99
Charnock, Robert 66
Charon 33, 99
Chatham 8, 69
Christian, Fletcher 88
Clarke, Frances 37
Clevely, John 12, 16, 38
Clinton 56, 100
Clive, Robert 41, 42
Colchester 17, 18, 19, 99
Commissioners of Bankruptcy 35
Comte De Florentine 24
Conder, Deborah 11, 85
Conqueror 23, 24, 70, 99
Conquistador 48
Constitution 67
Contest 63, 99
Cook, Capt James 19
Cormorant 30, 32, 34, 35, 99
Cornwall 70, 99
Cornwall, Capt Fredrick 19
Cornwallis, General 33, 35, 52
Cotton, Sir Evan 43
Court of Chancery 39, 60
Courtauld, Samuel 77, 78
Cramer, Mark 46, 101
Crash 63, 99
Cubitt, Alexander 82

D

Dawes 37
Declaration of Independence 30, 33
Defoe, Daniel 36, 38, 45
Deptford 4, 15, 20, 21, 35, 36, 37, 38, 39, 40, 45, 46, 47, 49, 50, 51, 52, 53, 55, 57, 63, 64, 66, 68, 69, 71, 73, 74, 75, 81, 90, 91, 93, 102
Devonshire 70, 99
Dews, Nathaniel 51
Diamond 59, 99

Diligence 69
Dorsetshire 66, 94, 100
Dragon 21
Druid 23, 99
Dryad 59, 61, 62, 99
Dudman, John 45, 47, 58, 59, 60, 69
   " , William 2, 23, 27, 29, 37, 38, 39, 43, 45, 46, 47, 60
Dummer, Edmund 6
Dundas, Capt George 102
Dunira 72, 100
Dunkirk 25, 37
Durand, J 48, 100
Dutton 56, 57, 100
Dyer, Joseph 48

E

Eagle 17, 19, 20, 21, 99
Earl Fitzwilliam 56, 100
Earl St Vincent 66, 100
East India Company, Hon 1, 2, 4, 5, 37, 38, 41, 43, 46, 51
Edwards, Capt 88
Elk 63, 99
Enfield 56, 100
Eolus 63, 99
Esdale, Peter 56
Evelyn Estates 38, 39
Experiment 47, 55, 99

F

Fairford 56, 100
Fairy 62
Falcon 11, 99
Farmer, Capt 24
Farquharson, Capt James 11, 17, 55, 56, 100, 101
Farrington, Capt William 56, 100
Forrester, Lord 14
Fox 20
Fuller, Col 11

G

General Barker 48, 100
General Coate 56, 100
George II 5, 20, 26, 27, 29, 30
George III 24, 27, 29
Gibraltar 13, 21, 25
Glorious First of June 51, 63, 76
Gloucester 15
Gooday, Edmund 10, 11
   " , William 85
Gordon, Rev William 27, 28
Gosfield Hall 74, 75, 76, 77, 78, 79, 81, 98

Granado 11, 16, 99
Granby 46, 100
Grove St Yard 38, 39, 40, 47, 54, 55, 58
Gunfleet Sands 21

H
H.M. Customs 57
Hamaoze 24
Hamilton, William 66
Hampshire 11, 15, 16, 99
Hannibal 70
Harrier 63, 99
Harwich 17, 99
Harwich 2, 14, 15, 16, 17, 18, 19, 20,
    21, 22, 23, 25, 26, 28, 31, 32, 33, 34,
    35, 37, 38, 40, 46, 54, 76, 87, 99
Hastings, Warren 41
Hector 46, 47, 50, 55, 99
Hellyer, Mr 31
Henry VIII 5, 7
Hinchbrook 56, 100
Hindustan I 56, 57, 100
Hindustan II 66, 100
Hotham, Richard 48, 49, 56, 90, 101
Hound 47, 55, 99
Hydra 47, 48, 99
Hythe 72, 100

I
Inconstant 51, 53, 99
Inflexible 33, 34, 99
Ipswich 1, 8, 9, 10, 11, 12, 14, 15, 16,
    18, 23, 27, 29, 34, 35, 37, 38, 39, 40,
    76, 81, 83, 84, 85
Iris 51, 99
Irresistible 33, 35, 54, 99

J
James, Sir William 56, 100
Jenkins' Ear, War of 13, 17
John's Ness 15, 16, 33

K
Kentish Knock 18
King John 8
King's Yard, Harwich 6, 14, 17, 23, 30,
    33, 37, 68
Kite 59, 99

L
La Piémontaise 66, 81, 94, 95
La Prosperine 61
Landguard Fort 21
Lane, Thomas 46, 56, 101
Langston, Rev John 11

Larkins, John P. 66, 100, 101
    " , William 55, 56, 100, 101
Leopard 15
Levant 45, 46
Litchfield 99
Liverpool, Earl of 72
Locke, John 66, 101
Locust 63, 99
Lord Lowther 72, 100
Lord Nelson 66, 100
Lowestoft 1, 8, 18, 81, 82, 83

M
Madras 56, 101
Majestic 51, 52, 53, 54, 99
Mallard 63, 99
Margarite and Ann 56
Marlborough 70, 99
Marquis of Lansdown 56, 100
Marquis of Wellington 72, 100
Mars 56, 100
Marshalsea Gaol 19
Mary Rose 47, 88
Maskelyne, Nevil DD FRS 48, 90
Mecklenburg, Princess Charlotte of
    26, 27, 28
Meeting House, Butt Lane 61, 69
Melville Castle 56, 100
Mercury 23, 99
Metcalf 66, 100
Middlesex 56, 100
Moddat, Andrew 56
Modiste 56
Morocco 20
Mount Stuart 48, 100
Munro, Major Sir Henry 42

N
Napoleon Bonaparte 5, 64, 70, 71, 93
National Maritime Museum 1, 56, 92,
    107
Navy Board 2, 3, 4, 6, 7, 11, 14, 15, 17,
    18, 19, 20, 21, 22, 23, 24, 25, 26, 30,
    31, 32, 34, 35, 39, 40, 45, 46, 47, 48,
    52, 53, 54, 55, 59, 61, 62, 63, 64, 68,
    69, 70, 71, 73
Nelson, Admiral Lord 14, 70
Neptune 56
Nesbit, Albert 46, 101
Newte, Thomas 56
Nightingale 48
Nile, Battle of the 63, 76
Nonsuch 15
Northumberland 63, 64, 65, 99
Notcutt, Anne 11

Notcutt, Rev William 11
Nova Scotia Shipyard 23, 24, 26, 27,
    33, 37

O
Ogilby, John 9
Orion 51, 52, 53, 56, 99
Orpheus 30, 32, 48, 51, 55, 99
Orwell 83, 84
Ostend 21

P
Pactolus 70, 71, 99
Palmer, William 56
Pandora 47, 48, 55, 81, 88, 99
Paris, Peace of 29, 45
Parthian 70, 99
Pelican 47, 55, 99
Pellew, Edward 56
Pennington, Joseph 9
Phoenix 66, 101
Pitt, William the Elder 24, 29, 66
Plymouth Sound 24, 56, 57
Ponsbourne 46, 56
Portmahon 14
Preneuse 53
Preston 66, 101
Prince Regent 72, 101
Prince Wm. Henry 56, 101
Princep, John 66
Princess Amelia 56
Princess Amelia II 44, 72, 101
Proserpine 33, 34, 99

Q
Quebec 23, 24, 26, 27, 99
Queen Elizabeth I 41, 51, 98
Queensland Museum 88, 89

R
Ramsay, George 48, 56
Ravensbury Manor House 63, 70, 93
Raymond, Charles 43, 46
Repulse 63, 99
Resolution 46, 101
Rice, Capt Henry 56, 100
River Orwell 8, 9, 11, 17, 20, 21, 23,
    83, 84
River Thames 24, 27, 29, 36, 38, 39, 40,
    44, 45, 46, 49, 52, 55, 73, 76, 90, 93
Roberts, Mr 63, 64, 69, 70, 71, 73, 74
Robust 23, 24, 26, 27, 99
Rockingham 56, 101
Rodney 70, 99
Rose 14, 25, 47, 88

Rotherhithe 21, 71, 73, 75,
Royal Admiral 48, 63, 64, 101
Royal Bishop 48, 101
Royal Charlotte 46, 101
Royal Charlotte II 46
Royal Dockyards 5, 6, 14, 15, 19, 24,
    33, 37, 39, 45, 69
Royal Dockyard, Deptford 15, 37, 38,
    39, 69
    " , Plymouth 37
    " , Portsmouth 37
    " , Woolwich 23, 25, 37, 69
Royal Henry 46, 101
Royal Oak 70
Royal Sovereign 19

S

Savage 33, 99
Scarborough 14
Scipio 51, 55, 99
Seahorse 99
Septre 69
Seven Years War 22, 23, 30, 37, 45, 70
Severn 17, 99
Sir William Pultney 66, 101
Skottowe, Nicholas 56, 100
Slade, Sir Thomas 14, 15, 16, 17, 20, 24
Solebay 51, 99
Southwold 8, 83
Spanker 59, 60, 99
Speaker 27, 29, 37, 38, 101
Speed, John 9
Speedwell 25
Spiteful 63, 99
St Clement's Churchyard 85

St Clement's Yard 8, 9, 11, 14, 15, 16,
    23
St Helena 64, 65, 66
Success 14
Sulivan 56, 101
Sultan 30, 31, 46, 70, 99
Surveillante 24, 26
Susanna 37
Sutherland 15
Sylph 59, 99

T

Tacket Street 8, 11, 27, 37, 85, 107
Taunton Castle 56, 101
Terrible 23, 27, 99
Terror 23, 99
Thames II 72, 101
The Nore 18, 19
Thomas, James 66, 100
Thornhill, Sir Thomas 8
Thos Coutts 72, 74, 101
Tiger 17
Tortoise 51, 99
Trafalgar, Battle of 64, 76
Tremendous 51, 52, 53, 99
Triton 63, 65, 99
Trowbridge, Admiral 17
Turner, John 23, 25, 26, 31, 32
Tuscany Frigate 37

U

Ushant 24
Utrecht, Treaty of 12

V

Vansittart, Rt Hon 72, 73
Varunna 66, 101
Versailles, Peace of 52
Vestal 23, 99
Victory 14, 62

W

Walmer Castle 66, 101
Walpole, Horace 13
Warren Hastings I 56, 101
Warren Hastings II 66, 67, 101
Warren Hastings III 94
Waterloo, Battle of 64, 71
Webster, David 56, 100
Wedderbourn, John 56, 100
Wellington 72
Wentworth, Sir Thomas 98
William Pitt 66, 101
Williams, Capt Henry 56
Williams, Robert 44, 48, 55, 56, 66, 72,
    94, 100, 101
Winchester 21
Windsor 72
Winterton 56, 81, 101, 102, 103
Wix Bishop 8, 11
Wood, John 46, 100

Y

Yarmouth Roads 20
York 48, 49, 63, 64, 90, 91, 99

Z

Zealous 51, 52, 53, 99
Zebra 33, 34, 99
Zephyr 47, 99